ncil for
cement
upport
ucation

DEVELOPING AN EFFECTIVE MAJOR GIFT PROGRAM:
From Managing Staff to Soliciting Gifts

Roy Muir and Jerry May, Editors

ISBN 0-89964-302-7

Printed in the United States of America.
Reprinted 1998, 2000.

Council for Advancement and Support of Education (CASE) is
the international education association serving professionals in the
disciplines of alumni relations, communications, and philanthropy.

CASE offers high-quality training, information resources, and a
wide variety of books, videotapes, and materials for advancement
professionals.

Visit our CASE Books catalog online at *www.case.org/books.*
To receive our printed catalog, call (202) 328-2273.

Book design: Ann M. Williams
Editor: Anne Kenealy

CASE. Books

1307 New York Avenue, NW
Suite 1000
Washington, DC 20005-4701

Dedicated to

Anita Miller Muir
1945 - 1993

Spouse and Partner to One

Friend and Colleague to the Other

Consummate Professional to Both

Contents

Figures

Foreword

ASE is pleased to present *Developing an Effective Major Gift Program: From Managing Staff to Soliciting Gifts,* a comprehensive guide to establishing new major gift programs and improving existing ones. We believe that this book will provide development professionals with a solid foundation of information with which they can develop and keep a strong base of major gift support. In today's competitive fund-raising climate, securing major gifts has become the principal means to meet the increasing financial needs of institutions, especially in an uncertain economic environment. Major gifts can mean the difference between an imperiled cash flow and the constancy of firm revenue.

Major gifts do not usually comprise the first step in an institution's fund-raising program. Nevertheless, cultivating these significant gifts can (and often does) provide the financial strength that secures an institution's future. In the scope of the development endeavor, major gifts are not only the sign of a mature and well-planned development operation—they are the mark of an institution that is "going places" in an impressive, dynamic, and sustainable way.

Developing an Effective Major Gift Program: From Managing Staff to Soliciting Gifts brings together in one resource years of major gift experience and wisdom from a distinguished group of CASE members. With a mixture of know-how, expertise, savvy, and grace, these authors convey their proven methods for cultivating major gifts.

CASE heartily thanks Roy Muir of the University of Michigan and Jerry May of Ohio State University for their inspiring and tireless efforts in creating and developing this book. Without their commitment, this distillation of the expertise and knowledge from the best and the brightest of the major gift fund-raising community would never have been possible. We thank the 18 authors featured in this book for contributing their timely and valuable insight. By sharing their professional successes, as well as mistakes, they have transformed an often forbidding challenge into an essential asset for the future well-being of society's most important institutions.

Peter McE. Buchanan
CASE President
December 1993

Preface

We are pleased to present this publication to our colleagues in the advancement community. We believe it is an excellent current and creative guide for development professionals. Our goal was to produce a useful, appealing publication that would guide and inspire advancement professionals and educational institutions in managing, planning, and establishing major gift programs. *Developing an Effective Major Gift Program: From Managing Staff to Soliciting Gifts* is a valuable assembly of the principles and practices from some of the finest professionals in the business today.

Major gift fund raising has become an essential component of a well-balanced and effective advancement program. Along with annual giving and planned giving, major gifts provide opportunities for institutions to maximize their philanthropic support.

An institution's advancement program should be a comprehensive endeavor. It should encourage individuals, over their lives, to contribute funds to the institution through a full spectrum of support including:

1. annual gifts from their income to provide for ongoing operating expenses;
2. large, significant gifts from time to time throughout their lives to support a special program, facility, or endowment need; and
3. a portion of their lifetime resources through an estate plan.

Major gift fund-raising programs focus on the middle portion of that spectrum: those occasional gifts that are significantly larger than annual support gifts, and that are generally given out of principal assets rather than from income.

As major gift programs have grown in educational advancement during the past couple of decades, we have learned a great deal about the most effective ways to organize and carry them out. This book presents the views and recommendations of leading professionals from some of the most successful major gift programs in North America. We believe these professionals, and the ideas they have conveyed here, provide a solid overview for establishing and managing a successful major gift program.

The editors have been honored to work with these exceptional colleagues and with CASE staff in bringing these principles and guidelines together. In addition, we are grateful to some especially wise and helpful colleagues. Chris Withers, associate vice president for development at the University of Richmond, and A.H. "Bud" Edwards, vice chancellor for advancement at the University of Arkansas, provided invaluable critical review of the book as it developed. Long-time colleague and advancement communicator Dennis Caplis served as our "great organizer." His work helped us immeasurably in establishing practice and principle among ourselves and the authors.

Again, we are pleased and excited to have brought together this excellent collaborative effort of insightful individuals. We are sure that you will find many useful guidelines, helpful ideas, and golden nuggets of inspiration in these pages. Whether you seek to improve your existing program or face the daunting task of establishing a major gift effort from scratch, we urge you to review these chapters carefully. We wish you the best of luck in your endeavor.

Roy Muir
Associate Vice President for Development
University of Michigan

Jerry May
Vice President for Development
Ohio State University
December 1993

Chapter 1

An Introduction to the Major Gift Process

Jon Cosovich
Vice President for Development
University of Michigan
Ann Arbor, Michigan

More and more institutions are turning to private giving to secure the financial resources necessary to fulfill their purpose. Museums, orchestras, performing artists, countless social service organizations, and educational institutions from kindergarten to postgraduate higher education increasingly rely on voluntary support from the private sector to sustain, improve, and expand their contributions to society.

Fund raising for private gifts is a fundamental part of the financial strategy for all institutions, both public and private. Changing economic circumstances and the blurring of the fiscal profile of both private and public institutions has made private sector support an absolute necessity for almost all institutions.

The single most important component of any educational institution's development strategy is major gift fund raising. Experience tells us that 80 percent of the dollars raised by institutions comes from a relatively small number of donors, the donors who make major gifts.

Individuals, of course, are not the only source of major gifts. Corporations and foundations can play an important role in any major gift development effort. However, it is individuals, contributing their own money, who have been the primary source of major gifts for educational institutions.

As we look to the future, we believe that individuals will continue to be the primary source of major gift support for institutions. We also believe that the fund-raising efforts of institutions can have the greatest impact, in terms of both level and purpose of giving, on individual major gift donors.

What is a major gift?

In answering that question we can only hide behind the fund raiser's theory of relativity: what constitutes a major gift depends very much on where you are standing in time and space. A small school that is just starting to solicit private support might consider a $20,000 donation to be a major gift. As the school's fund-raising program matures, the threshold level for a major gift might rise to $40,000. At a large university with a history of substantial private support and a sophisticated development program, the major gift range might start at $500,000. Other colleges and universities consider $100,000 as a starting level for major gifts.

Though the dollar amount of a major gift may vary from institution to institution, all major gifts share a common characteristic: major gifts have a significant impact on the giving area or purpose to which they are directed. For example, the major gift supporting a professorship should provide substantial support for that faculty position. A major gift supporting a fellowship should underwrite the majority of a student's costs. If the gift is made to help fund a facility, the major gift should be large enough to finance an important component of the building. Most schools, regardless of size, can use the impact of a gift to set the ranges of their major gift levels.

Who are major gift donors?

The "impact criterion" can also be used as a general qualification for major gift prospects. Prospects are those individuals with the capacity to provide a gift that will have a significant impact on a particular area of your institution. Within any group of prospects, there will be a wide variance of financial circumstance. For some prospects, making a major gift will be a once-in-a-lifetime commitment involving an important portion of their total assets. Other donors may not have accumulated significant wealth, but possess a high enough yearly income to undertake a major commitment. Other prospects may possess substantial wealth, and may provide several increasingly larger major gifts during their lifetimes.

What institutional support does a major gift program need?

A successful major gift program requires several prerequisites:
- leadership from the governing board;
- trust and confidence in the president;
- a coherent vision for the future of the institution;
- a clear development plan for realizing this vision; and
- a compelling statement of why private gifts are essential to implementing the development plan.

The institution must be fiscally responsible and well-managed. Possessing such a reputation will assure donors that their money will be used wisely and effectively.

Building major gift relationships requires time and teamwork. The major gift officer may take the lead in involving donors in the life of the school, but it takes the cooperation and participation of faculty, staff, and university management to make this involvement meaningful and rewarding. Moreover, the institution must regard the major gift process not merely as an exercise in asking for large sums of money, but as a process for building long-term relationships with donors.

How does the major gift program fit into the overall development effort?

To be most productive, a major gift program must be carefully and closely integrated with the other components of a comprehensive development effort. A successful major gift program cannot exist in isolation.

The link between an annual giving system and a major gift program illustrates just how important "development shop" interactions can be to overall program success. Annual giving is the primary avenue by which most donors come to include a college or university in their giving plans. If the annual giving program treats prospective donors badly, they will be unlikely to maintain or increase their giving. A sound annual giving program creates an atmosphere that encourages donors' increased involvement with and support for an institution.

Most successful major gift programs try to keep staff turnover to a minimum. Donors and staff invest time and energy in nurturing the donor/institution relationship. Although the donor's most important relationship is with the institution, that relationship is inextricably linked to the donor's relationship with the major gift officer. Asking donors to start new relationships with new staff people every year or two can kill the momentum and quality of your major gift program.

Science and art

One additional prerequisite for a successful major gift program is the effective blending of the science and the art of fund raising. The science of fund raising works to develop and operate various systems for:
- gathering and disseminating information on prospects;
- planning, coordinating, and implementing solicitations;
- ensuring proper recognition; and
- allocating stewardship responsibilities.

These systems give development officers the information and support they need to practice the art of major gift fund raising.

The art of fund raising is the ingredient that creates long-term relationships with donors. Different major gift prospects may have particularly strong beliefs, multiple interests, or established philanthropic priorities. You may need to employ uncommon flexibility, particular sensitivity, and boundless creativity to construct a gift opportunity that matches donor priorities with the needs and objectives of the institution.

Some donors respond to deference, others to aggressiveness. Each relationship will be unique and change over time. A successful major gift program builds a common foundation of honesty, integrity, and respect for confidentiality under every donor relationship. Such a foundation shows donors that, ethically, professionally, and practically, our institutions are worthy of support.

3

Conclusion

In today's competitive fund-raising environment, losing any momentum in your major gift program will make securing major gifts doubly difficult. Organizations and institutions in virtually every sector of society—the arts, social services, medical services, and education—have established fund-raising programs to increase their private support. To succeed in this environment, development officers must organize a major gift program systematically, manage donor relations artfully, and sustain gifts thoughtfully.

Chapter 2

Strategic Management Of a Major Gift Program

David R. Dunlop
Director of Capital Projects
Cornell University
Ithaca, New York

A t institution after institution, and in campaign after campaign, a pattern of giving is clear: the gifts of a very few donors account for a disproportionately large share of the total amount given. Once called the "20/80 rule" of fund raising, this phenomenon anticipated that 20 percent of the givers would provide 80 percent of the amount given. Now some fund raisers are starting to speak of a "10/90 rule" and even a "5/95 rule." I know one fund-raising consultant who found that 2.5 percent of the givers to his clients' institutions provided 98 percent of the total dollars given. These patterns of giving are not surprising; they reflect the uneven distribution of wealth in our society. What is surprising is that fund raisers have not given more of their attention to this most productive area of fund raising.

Extensive gift potential assessment programs and well-executed feasibility studies notwithstanding, even the best informed schools, colleges, and universities have only a partial knowledge of the wealth of their best prospects, and of their prospects' inclination to give from that wealth to their institution. If, by some miracle, each institution could know the total wealth of its constituents, most would discover that a few individuals were financially capable of making gifts of a size that could dramatically affect their institution's future.

Because major gifts have the potential to profoundly transform an institution, they merit a special kind of fund raising. This special fund raising for very large gifts is different from other forms of fund raising. At the same time, it is intimately involved with the other forms of fund raising and dependent upon them for much of its success.

The largest gifts an institution hopes to receive are often called by different names. Some institutions call them *special gifts, leadership gifts,* or *principal gifts.* In this book, we refer to these gifts as *major gifts* and *principal gifts.* What we call this class of gifts is not important, however. What is important is that both volunteers and staff professionals understand how making such gifts is experienced by the people giving them, and the fund-raising behaviors that are most appropriate to encourage those gifts.

Defining and understanding major gifts

A deeper understanding of major gift fund raising begins with the development of a more precise understanding of what a major gift is. Almost everyone acknowledges that what constitutes a major gift for one institution may be far different from what constitutes a major gift for another institution. But just what defines a major gift for your institution?

Some would define a major gift simply by its size. While this definition enjoys the virtue of simplicity, it is not an adequate definition for an institution that is undertaking a serious effort in major gift fund raising. Moreover, this definition is limited because it does not address the perspective of the major donor.

If the truth be told, there is no agreement among those who make gifts and the institutions that receive them as to what size of gift constitutes a major gift. To resolve that inconsistency we could simply say that major gifts are the category of gifts that are the largest a charitable institution hopes to receive.

Even if this definition provides a clear range by which to measure major gifts for a specific charitable institution, we are still faced with the problem that making gifts of that size may be a routine matter for some givers and a once-in-a-lifetime experience for others.

It is not the size of the gift that determines the most appropriate method of fund raising. Rather, it is the character of the giver's experience in making the gift that determines the most appropriate method of fund raising to use. Therefore, it is more functional to define the types of gifts we seek from the giver's experience than from the institution's perspective.

Nevertheless, many institutions define the gifts they seek in terms of amounts that are in proportion to their needs or experience. For example, a college might define a major gift as being in the range of $100,000 and up, $1 million and up, or $5 million and up, depending on what in the institution's experience seemed "major." Based upon its own definition, the school, college, or university would then establish a fund-raising program to encourage gifts at the major gift level. This type of major gift program focuses its attention on the constituents who are thought to be capable and likely to give a major gift.

The risk in defining and organizing a major gift program by the size of gift is that the program is deemed appropriate only for prospects who can give gifts of that size. For some prospects, making such a large gift may be a once-in-a-lifetime experience. For other prospects it may be an experience they will have over and over again.

Recently, an alumna of my university died, leaving virtually her whole estate to our alma mater. For 30 years I observed the experiences that led her to commit all that she had to our university. Earlier, another alumnus made a similar gift. For him the gift was but one of many of that size that he expected to make to our university and to other causes. To the university that received them, both were major gifts, though the commitment they reflected and the experiences that led to their being made were quite different.

The fund-raising principles that encourage a once-in-a-lifetime gift are different from those that encourage a gift of similar size that a person may make a number of times. As a result, a single major gift program may use two or more approaches in seeking gifts of approximately the same amount.

Most experienced laypeople and professional development officers treat each prospective major gift donor individually. However, many major gift programs employ fund-raising methods that do not respect each individual's different and very personal giving requirements.

Gifts from the donor's perspective

To think and speak more appropriately about the requirements of major gift fund raising we need to define gifts by the giver's experience, not only by their dollar amount. From the perspective of the giver there are three different types of gifts:

Regular gifts. These are gifts that a person makes repeatedly to the same cause. A giver might give a weekly donation to a church or synagogue, a quarterly donation to a public television station, or an annual gift to an alma mater. The giver makes regular gifts because he or she has made a similar gift to a specific cause in the past, and anticipates giving to it again in the future. The calendar plays an important part in the timing of regular gifts.

Special gifts. These gifts are often made to the same charitable institutions to which a giver makes regular gifts, but are frequently five or 10 times larger. Givers usually make special gifts in response to a special need, such as a church needing a new roof or a college adding a wing on its library. Special gifts are usually timed to the needs of the institution.

Ultimate gifts. Some people arrive at a special time in life when they contemplate how to best disperse their accumulated wealth. In such contemplation an individual thinks not only of family and friends, but also of the institutions they cherish. When these individuals seriously contemplate the final disposition of their wealth, they often decide to make one or more ultimate gifts. Such commitments are frequently 1,000 times and even 10,000 times larger than the regular gifts the same individuals make to the same cause. Ultimate gifts are rarely timed to the calendar or to the needs of the institution. Rather, the personal circumstances in the life of the giver most influence the timing of ultimate gifts.

Using fund-raising programs that match the gift

Just as the giver's experience defines several kinds of gifts, each kind of gift requires a specific type of fund-raising strategy.

Speculative fund raising. This method of fund raising focuses almost entirely on the process of asking for the gift. Speculative fund raising is based on the premise that if enough people are asked to give, a sufficient number will respond positively to make the whole effort worthwhile. This development strategy invests little in developing an individual's sense of commitment. Direct mail appeals, telethons, and phonathons are examples of speculative fund raising. Even personal solicitations can be speculative, such as when volunteers solicit prospective givers whose readiness to give is unknown. Speculative fund raising is most appropriately used in the pursuit of regular gifts.

Campaign and project fund raising. As the size of a gift sought increases from regular to special, so must the solicitor's investment in developing the prospective donor's readiness to give. In campaign/project fund raising, as much as half of the fund-raising efforts may be invested in helping the prospect develop a sense of commitment to the cause. While asking for the gift is still an important part of campaign/project fund raising, the development of the prospective giver's readiness to give receives much more attention.

Nurturing fund raising. Ultimate gifts require a method of fund raising that emphasizes nurturing the relationship between the giver and the institution. Nurturing fund raising focuses on building the prospective giver's sense of commitment to both the institution and the purpose of the gift.

Ultimate gifts are not timed to the calendar or even to the needs of the institution, but to the giver's readiness to make an ultimate disposition of his or her wealth. Therefore, there is little even the most sophisticated asking can do to accelerate a person's readiness to make a once-in-a-lifetime decision. Nurturing fund raising works to build the ultimate donor's inclination to give, so that when that friend contemplates making an ultimate gift, yours will be the institution he or she will choose to support.

What motivates the major donor to give?

While the specific experiences that lead a person to make an ultimate gift are usually unique to the individual, the types of experiences that have led people to make such gifts are often the same. These common types of experiences have to do with the prospective giver's:
- awareness;
- understanding;
- caring;
- involvement;
- sense of commitment; and
- expression of commitment.

One of America's great fund raisers, G. Taylor (Buck) Smith, described some of these same elements in his "Five I's of Fund Raising," which he identifies as:
1. identification;
2. information;
3. interest;
4. involvement; and
5. investment.

Regular gifts and ultimate gifts are made for a number of divergent reasons. However, it is almost always a personal and deep sense of commitment that motivates the giver to make an ultimate gift. This commitment has been nurtured by experiences that developed the giver's *awareness, understanding, caring, involvement,* and *sense of commitment.*

If we want to receive our friends' ultimate expressions of philanthropy, we must provide those friends with opportunities to develop their awareness, understanding, caring, involvement, and sense of commitment to our institutions and activities. It is this investment of time and effort that distinguishes major gift fund raising from other forms of fund raising. Consequently, the process of major gift fund raising may be thought of as looking something like this:

Figure 2-1: The major gift fund-raising process

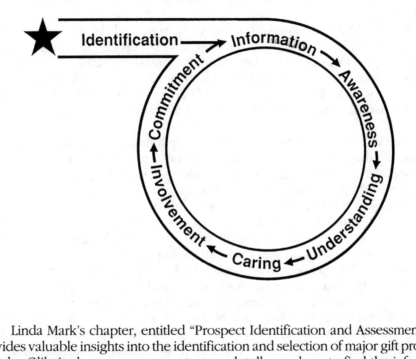

Linda Mark's chapter, entitled "Prospect Identification and Assessment," provides valuable insights into the identification and selection of major gift prospects. John Gliha's chapter on prospect research tells you how to find the information you need to take appropriate major gift initiatives. Once you have identified and researched your prospects, you will be ready to start the initiatives to cultivate each prospect.

Nurturing the major gift

Many fund-raising programs ask members of a major gift committee, volunteers, or staff members to solicit major gift prospects. While this is appropriate in speculative and campaign/project fund raising, it is not the way to proceed if your objective is a prospect's ultimate gift.

In nurturing fund raising for ultimate gifts, the people who can most effectively conceive, plan, and execute initiatives to develop a prospect's awareness, understanding, caring, involvement, and commitment are those friends who are already the natural partners in the prospect's relationship with the institution. Consequently, nurturing fund raising focuses not on *assigning* or *volunteering* responsibility for a cultivating a prospect, but on *discovering* the individuals through whom the prospect relates to the institution. Such individuals can, in a climate of comfort and confidence, help draw the prospect closer to the institution.

Buck Smith calls these natural partners, who are in the best position to help develop major gift relationships, the *primes*. Other individuals, who are also willing and able to nurture the relationship, he calls *secondaries*. A prime or secondary may be an alumnus, a trustee, a faculty member, the president of the institution, or a student. Primes and secondaries are individuals who can, through their own personal contacts, strengthen the bond between a prospect and an institution.

It should be noted that the terms prime and secondary are usually reserved for use within the institution and among fund-raising staff. Volunteers should seldom be called or encouraged to think of themselves as being prime or secondary individuals. More likely, they would think of themselves as simply helping the institution through their connection with a philanthropic friend.

Primes and secondaries often lead busy lives that may already be full of demands competing for their time and attention. It is the staff manager's role to support, facilitate, and stimulate initiatives of these important individuals on behalf of the institution. The prime and secondary individuals and the staff manager work as a team to draw a prospect closer to the institution and to develop his or her sense of commitment. This team also targets the giving purposes that the prospect will find most appealing. One of the best ways to establish this coordinated effort is by adhering to a simple six-step discipline developed by Buck Smith. This discipline is called the "moves concept" of major gift fund raising.

"Moving" a major gift fund-raising program

The "moves concept" recommends that the staff manager, in consultation with the appropriate primes and secondaries, take the following six steps for each major gift prospect every few weeks:

1. Review the conversations and activities that have occurred with the prospect.
2. Plan and set priorities for next steps.
3. Coordinate all individuals who are involved with the prospect.
4. Execute the initiative.
5. Evaluate the effect of the initiative.
6. Report and record the results of the initiative.

These six steps do not, in and of themselves, constitute an initiative or "move" to build awareness, understanding, caring, involvement, or commitment. Rather, these steps make up a sound procedure for generating such initiatives.

Essential initiatives for the major gift program

Two types of initiatives work to accomplish major gift objectives. One type of initiative is conceived, planned, and executed for a specific prospective giver. Such an initiative is called a *foreground initiative*. The other type of initiative is conceived, planned, and executed for groups of potential givers, among whom may be one or more major gift prospects. This is known as a *background initiative*. The staff manager, working with the appropriate primes and secondaries, is responsible for undertaking the appropriate foreground and background initiatives.

More essentials for success

Although an institution may rely heavily on the principles of nurturing fund raising to guide its major gift efforts, there are other essential elements for success that merit attention. Key to the success of nurturing fund raising are the quality, frequency, and continuity of the initiatives taken with each prospect. Fund-raising efforts must focus on the "right prospects." And, these prospects must be given opportunities to express their growing sense of commitment in more than just financial ways.

Quality. Assuring the quality and appropriateness of initiatives taken is the first essential. Occasionally, the zeal of development officers and volunteers leads them to take initiatives that are out of keeping with the nature of the prospect/ institution relationship. For example, the birthday card that I receive from a local insurance salesperson, who really does not know me, makes me think twice about the birthday cards sent to prospects on behalf of my institution. Such initiatives, no matter how well intended, can harm the giver/institution relationship. Such inappropriate gestures make the sender and the institution seem "on the make" and insincere.

When selecting appropriate initiatives to build your institution's friendships, you should apply the same standards you would use in your personal friendships. In other words, if you would not feel comfortable taking a particular proposed action with a personal friend, you should not try it on an institutional friend either. You must also make sure that your institution's stream of initiatives include active as well as passive initiatives. It is fine to keep friends informed, but they also need to be actively involved.

Frequency. The second essential of a nurturing fund-raising strategy is the frequency of initiatives. Unless a prospective giver enters into the life of the institution with some frequency, it is unlikely that this friend will direct his or her ultimate gift to your institution. Consequently, the staff manager must work with the primes and secondaries to ensure that the institution is in touch with prospective givers every few weeks, and certainly no less frequently than once a month. Major gift fund raisers should perform Buck Smith's six-step discipline for each ultimate gift prospect at least once a month or more frequently, if possible.

Continuity. Besides assuring the quality and frequency of initiatives, you should work to ensure the continuity of initiatives. Continuity must take into account any element that can develop a friend's sense of commitment to the institution and its work. I recommend using the diagram on page 9 as a guide to the types of initiatives that will provide continuity to your fund-raising strategy.

Focus. Institutions, like individuals, are limited in the number of genuine friendships they can sustain. Friendships can't be faked. They take time, talent, creativity, and other resources that are in limited supply. Just as an individual focuses on a few good friends, so too, must an institution. Because nurturing fund raising is, in essence, the thoughtful management of initiatives to express institutional friendship, it must focus on a few special friends.

Until you have become comfortable and effective with the discipline of nurturing fund raising, you should start your major gift initiative by focusing on as few as five prospects. Start with the five individuals who are most likely to give your institution major gifts. There will be time to add others later.

Three criteria can help you select the friends toward whom you should direct nurturing fund-raising strategies:
- financial capacity;
- interest or potential interest in the institution; and
- charitable nature.

Good prospect identification and assessment, as well as prospect research, will help you assess the first two criteria. Determining the third criterion will require using your special skills in relationship building and intuition.

Not all wealthy and interested constituents are charitably inclined. If you focus your major gift fund-raising efforts without considering an individual's charitable nature, you may waste your best efforts. But if you are able to identify prospective major donors who possess the capacity to give and have a charitable interest in your institution, you will enjoy an entirely different level of fund-raising efficiency.

Certainly a record of generous giving suggests a charitable nature. However, the absence of such a history of charitable giving does not necessarily preclude a charitable nature. Many well-known philanthropists did not begin their philanthropic efforts until after they retired from business. The recognition of a charitable nature may be the most important and the most difficult criterion to discern in the selection of major gift prospects. Nevertheless, your development effort's efficiency and success will depend on it.

Expression. Nurturing fund raising for ultimate gifts is concerned with developing attitudes and feelings as the means of obtaining dollars and cents. This type of development works to encourage the donor's sense of commitment to shared values and purposes. By considering the full range of beliefs, interests, and energy that each friend has to offer, nurturing fund raising does not limit its attention to the financial ability of the donor. Your institution must be prepared to welcome the moral, political, personal, and spiritual support of its friends as well.

Integrating with the rest of the development office

The concepts of nurturing fund raising are at the heart of major gift fund raising. However, your institution's efforts in annual giving, campaign fund raising, planned giving, and corporate and foundation fund raising will be just as critical to the success of your major gift program. Neither nurturing fund raising nor major gift fund raising can be effective when they work separately from the rest of an institution's development program.

Some development officers believe that major gift programs should operate independently from other fund-raising programs, because major gifts are often an institution's most important and sizable gifts. However, when major gift programs are separated from the whole, they run the risk of becoming competitive with the rest of an institution's development effort.

Nurturing fund raising and major gift programs benefit when coordinated with the rest of an institution's development activities. This integration guarantees that they will function in a complementary rather than a competitive way. For example, the promptness, warmth, and sincerity of a thank-you note for an annual fund gift may the best way to convey your institution's gratitude to a donor. These positive experiences develop and reinforce habits of giving.

Capital campaigns are another example of how nurturing fund raising depends on the work of others in the development office. The urgency of campaign fund raising often captures the attention of some of the institution's best prospects. When donors are asked for campaign gifts to meet specific needs of the institution, they also become aware, informed, and involved with the important work of the institution.

There are many ways to organize a successful major gift program that is integrated, coordinated, and complementary to the rest of the institution's fund-raising programs. However, it is important that related fund-raising staff understand the concepts of nurturing fund raising. For without the help and support of all of its colleagues, the institution's opportunity for successful nurturing fund raising is greatly diminished. Therefore, the development officer must be prepared to teach nurturing fund-raising skills to development staff, administrators, faculty, primes, and secondaries.

Organization. Many institutions ask the volunteers who are most helpful in encouraging and soliciting major gifts to serve on a *major gift committee*. While such committees can be a valuable asset, they also require a great deal of staff time and support. The premature organization of a major gift committee can siphon away the time and effort of both volunteers and staff. It can also take important resources away from the real work of managing appropriate initiatives. Therefore, you might want to postpone the organization of a major gift committee until the need for it is truly apparent or urgent. You will probably find that most major gift volunteers will not need to serve on a committee in order to help you with the major gift prospects they know.

While speculative fund raising and campaign/project fund raising use organizational structures for enlisting the help of volunteers, nurturing fund raising is different. Nurturing fund raising organizes its efforts by thoroughly and thoughtfully managing initiatives that build awareness, understanding, caring, involvement, and commitment with the quality, frequency, continuity, and focus that are essential for success.

You may not need to establish a committee to enlist help in taking those initiatives. Most of these are best done discreetly, and often involve only one or two individuals. Until there is a significant need to organize a major gift committee, it is more efficient to enlist the help you need on an ad hoc basis.

Who should do what?

Not everyone is suited to perform the same role in nurturing fund raising for major gifts. Some volunteers and staff, by virtue of their long-standing association with an institution and its friends, are well-suited to play a role in developing a prospect's relationship with the institution. Earlier in this chapter we identified these volunteers and staff as primes and secondaries.

Other individuals may lack knowledge and familiarity with an institution's major gift prospects, but have experience in the process of major gift fund raising. Their role, at least initially, should lie in helping with the organization and management of fund raising. This experience will help them earn the confidence and friendship of major gift prospects. With time, their role may change from being a manager and facilitator of major gift initiatives to being a prime or secondary.

Some individuals, by their nature or experience, are effective in the role of solicitor; others are not. It is important to respect the difference. Individuals who serve as a prime or secondary may never serve as the solicitor of the friends whose sense of commitment to the institution they helped develop.

Evaluating your major gift fund-raising program

The timing of bottom-line program evaluation that is based on the number and amount of gifts received differs for speculative, campaign/project, and nurturing fund raising. The success of speculative fund raising can only be judged at the end of the regular fund-raising interval. The end of the campaign or project is the judgement day for campaign/project fund raising.

In nurturing fund raising for ultimate gifts, bottom-line evaluation is appropriate only at the end of each prospect's life. Consequently, it would be inappropriate to gauge the success or failure of a major gift program, which is engaged in nurturing fund raising, by the number and amount of gifts received in a single year. During the course of a year, your initiatives may build strong relationships with major gift prospects, though your institution may not receive a single ultimate gift. Conversely, you may do a poor job in managing such initiatives, but may still receive several large ultimate gifts. These gifts usually result from prospect initiatives that your major gift staff made years or even decades earlier.

Of course, those who are responsible for nurturing fund raising usually cannot wait until their prospects die to evaluate the performance of their program. Many major gift programs examine the number and amount of gifts received over several years as one indication of the performance of their program. In addition, it is also a good idea to examine the initiatives taken with a sampling of major gift prospects to evaluate the current effectiveness of a major gift program.

In addition to their role in the management, coordination, communication, and stimulation of initiatives, tracking systems are also a primary resource for the evaluation of the initiatives taken with major gift prospects. The tracking systems discussed by Carole Karsch in the chapter entitled "Prospect Management: Co-ordination and Tracking" provide the kind of record of initiatives that is needed to conduct a thorough evaluation.

At least once a year you should examine your institution's major gift program with these eight questions in mind:

1. Are the initiatives taken with each major gift prospect consistent with the institution's strategic plan?

2. Has each major gift prospect been asked for an annual gift?

3. Has each major gift prospect received the quality, frequency, and continuity of initiatives required for the successful development of their awareness, under-standing, caring, involvement, and commitment?

4. Has there been an appropriate distribution of initiatives among the program's prospects?

5. Is the program focused on the correct prospects?

6. Is the program working with the optimal number of prospects?

7. Have the most appropriate primes and secondaries been identified for each prospect?

8. Is the staffing and budget of the program sufficient to support its gift potential?

What will a major gift program cost?

A major gift program engaged in nurturing fund raising is simultaneously the least expensive and the most expensive type of fund raising that an institution will conduct. Such a program is the least expensive in the cost per dollar raised, when compared to major gift programs that use other strategies. However, nurturing fund raising is most expensive in terms of the demands it places upon the non-financial resources of the institution, such as the time of its chief executive, trustees, faculty, and staff.

Budgeting for major gift programs is difficult because so much is at stake. Although there is no simple formula to follow in building a major gift program budget, it should be tailored to the needs and circumstances of the institution. Routine expenditures, such as staffing, facilities, equipment, and office supplies, are fairly easy to project. It is the exceptional expenses that make the accurate estimation of anticipated expense so difficult.

From time to time in the course of a major gift fund-raising plan, it may become necessary to charter planes, commission portraits, hold dedications, sponsor testimonial dinners, and take other very costly initiatives. Whether counted within the major gift program budget or outside of it, your development program must make provisions for these exceptional expenses when the best interest of the institution calls for them.

Matters of style

The requirement of good stewardship is not lessened by the size of the gifts a fund raiser seeks. While major gift fund raising may incur exceptional expenses that are in keeping with the lifestyle of our benefactors, it should not alter the frugal style with which the major gift staff conduct themselves. The accommodations you select, the cars you rent, the economy of your travel arrangements, and your office furnishings speak to your stewardship of the gifts you receive.

If you extend the hand of friendship in major gift fund raising based solely on an individual's capacity to give, you run the risk of appreciating people just because of their wealth. This is not an attractive trait for the fund raiser or the institution. The recognition of a prospect's wealth should be coupled with an appreciation of shared values and purposes. Relationships that are based solely on one dimension of a person's life are limited and often shallow. If our focus is based only on a person's wealth, we run the risk of stunting the relationship. For the sake of the relationship we must take the whole person into account and be interested in the non-financial contributions, as well as the financial gifts that our friends have to offer.

A kind and forgiving nature is a distinct asset for anyone engaged in major gift fund raising. A charitable nature that allows the major gift fund raiser to genuinely like a prospect in spite of his or her imperfections can make the difference between a sincere and an insincere relationship.

While the major gift fund raiser must focus time and attention on prospects for major gifts, the courtesy extended to other individuals of lesser means cannot be diminished. To do otherwise would reflect adversely on both the fund raiser and the institution.

Summary

While the specific experiences that lead a person to make an ultimate gift or other major gift may be unique to each individual, the types of experiences that lead donors to make such gifts are amazingly similar. These experiences develop the prospective major donor's awareness, understanding, caring, involvement, and commitment to the institution and the purpose of the gift. Nurturing fund raising seeks to give prospective major donors access to these experiences.

Initiatives to create these experiences fall into two categories: *foreground initiatives* that are conceived, planned, and executed with a specific individual in mind; and *background initiatives* that are conceived, planned, and executed with groups of prospects in mind. A *staff manager*, working in a team with *primes* and *secondaries*, conceives, plans, and executes foreground initiatives. This team also takes advantage of appropriate background initiatives to develop the prospect's sense of commitment to the institution and to seek the prospect's gifts.

By following a six-step discipline, your development effort can preserve the *quality, frequency*, and *continuity* of its initiatives. At least once a month the staff manager, in consultation with the appropriate primes and secondaries, *reviews, plans, coordinates, executes, evaluates*, and *records* the initiatives taken for each major gift prospect. A prospect tracking system is used to record and communicate the initiatives as they are planned and executed.

Initiatives that were launched years and even decades in the past are often the inspiration for major gifts that are made in the present. Such gifts are the stuff of a successful nurturing fund-raising approach. In the short term, the effectiveness of a major gift program is most appropriately gauged by an examination of the quality, frequency, and continuity of the initiatives taken with each prospect. Only in the long term will the number and amount of gifts received become a valid indicator of the program's strength.

The late Si Seymour used to say: "If you want to raise alfalfa you can get several crops a year. But if you want to raise oaks, it will take a little longer." Institutions that invest in major gift programs that include nurturing fund raising for ultimate gifts must be prepared to wait for the oaks to grow. While you wait, you may be pleasantly surprised by some fine crops of "annual fund alfalfa" or by harvests of special campaigns that were planted to meet the institution's most urgent needs.

Chapter 3

Developing Major Gift Staff

Carol L. O'Brien
President
Carol O'Brien Associates
Durham, North Carolina

"Faster than a speeding bullet . . . Able to leap tall buildings in a single bound . . . "

Qualities of an effective major gift staff

Career position descriptions in the *Chronicle of Higher Education* may lead readers to believe that many major gift officers need credentials akin to the fabled "superperson" heralded above in order to be recruited. The qualities and value of fine major gift staff are inestimable. However, the fund-raising environment in which that staff person will work is often the true determinant of the abilities that the major gift officer will need.

You should review the following factors, both in terms of your current situation and the fund-raising environment you may wish to create, to organize effective major gift staff:

1. Is the major gift officer viewed as an internal manager of a major gift program, a front-line fund raiser, or both?

2. Is this position one of the most senior in the organization, second perhaps to the director of development, or is it one of many mid-level positions in the organization?

3. Will the major gift officer function as a trainer, as well as a manager and development officer?

4. Besides the direct supervisor, who else will this person support in major gift initiatives (e.g., the president, the head, the chief development officer, trustees, deans, faculty, etc.)?

5. Will the person have access to experienced planned giving counsel and financial planning advice?

6. At what evolutionary phase is the major gift program: non-existent, emerging, or mature? Is there a "major gift culture" at the institution, or must the major gift officer articulate a philosophy for major gifts as well as direct or expand the program?

7. Are there organizational structures, such as a decentralized development program, that may influence the specific characteristics candidates should have?

This partial inventory will lead you to identify other considerations that are unique to your needs and expectations for major gift staff.

Although the majority of the following traits are desirable for all advancement professionals, they are vital for major gift staff:
- integrity, discretion, sincerity, and sensitivity;
- ability to listen, analyze, facilitate, and articulate;
- intelligence, maturity, flexibility, sense of humor, and a tolerance for ambiguity;
- patience and persistence;
- commitment to philanthropy, notable education, and ideally, to your institution;
- understanding of finances and ways of giving; and
- willingness to make the commitment to both the position and the organization requisite to building and sustaining relationships.

You may think that the "superperson" description would be easier to fill than this wish list. However, by starting with a strong grounding in the first three items, an individual can become a fine major gift officer. And, if I could choose only one trait, my vote would be for the *ability to listen*.

Staff training and growth

The orientation and training of a major gift officer has three parts:
- institutional knowledge;
- development principles and operations; and
- constituency knowledge.

Although it would be delightful if these areas could be quickly and effectively covered in the first few days that a new staff person was on the job, realistically the major gift officer should be committed to continuing education. The major gift staff member and his or her supervisor should agree on a plan for orientation and ongoing professional growth. The senior manager should actively participate in scheduling the orientation and debriefing the staff person on his or her progress.

Institutional knowledge. Many schools have established orientation programs that cover the following topics, both in written and oral presentations:
- academic strengths and traditions;
- admissions policies and trends;
- campus life issues, such as residential living, athletics, etc.;

• financial operations, including endowment policies, investment strategies, and budget;

• governance structure and by-laws;

• history of the founding of the institution, landmark institutional events, and personalities; and

• strategic planning and priority-setting procedures.

Since it is incumbent on a major gift officer to have excellent working relationships with key members of the faculty and administration, the orientation can provide an opportunity to meet these people, as well as understand the human dimension of the institution. In the early stages of the staff person's tenure, he or she should meet with colleagues in both academic and administrative roles. Given the hierarchical nature of some institutions, the supervisor may need to request these appointments.

Development principles and operations. If a major gift officer is new to an institution's development staff, he or she will want to become conversant with the scope of the program:

• all facets of individual giving, including prospect identification and research;

• institutional giving programs, such as foundation and corporate development; and

• professional support services, such as communications, events management, donor relations, and gift processing.

On any given day, a major gift officer will need to draw on the expertise of several areas. The staff person who demonstrates an early and sincere interest in learning about colleagues' responsibilities will increase the likelihood of positive responses to future requests for help or information. If a policy and procedures manual exists, refer to it. If it doesn't, question its absence.

A major gift officer should be cognizant of the organization's previous campaigns or project fund drives, including their goals, outcomes, and the roles that major gifts played in the success or failure of these initiatives.

Depending on the individual's experience, the major gift officer may benefit from courses in finance, public speaking, or writing.

Finally, the major gift officer needs to hone his or her skills in prospect management—the timely and sensitive orchestration of the prospective giver's relationship with the organization. Fortunately, within this book and in other articles, there is helpful codification of prospect management and principles of major or "ultimate" giving. However, it is sometimes difficult for a major gift staff member to see how to apply these principles in a given setting.

Staff participation in the major gift experience. Perhaps the best way for major gift staff, indeed for staff responsible for any level of capital giving, to develop skills in prospect management is to learn from experience. In this case, the experience from which they can learn is that of other able major gift officers or senior development professionals.

When our firm conducts major gift training, we invariably use a *case study method.* We tailor hypothetical situations to the issues and personalities represented in the client's experience. Participants—be they staff or volunteers—analyze specific cases and plan a strategy for involvement and solicitation.

This approach can certainly be utilized for in-house training as well. Case studies recount the actual events and decisions that prompted individuals to become involved meaningfully in an organization. They also help development staff to understand the motivations that stimulated donors to give. Case studies prompt staff to examine giving patterns and other donor-related issues. For example, how vital is recognition, both by peers and in a tangible form, to the prospective giver? Who are the decision makers in a gift commitment? How do we learn about areas or relationships that are important to the donor?

Staff/donor interactions. As the major gift staff member becomes acclimated to your organization and his or her assigned prospects, it is vital that the supervisor create opportunities for natural interaction between the staff person and these prospects. Some ways to facilitate these relationships include:

• invitations to major donor dinners, receptions, and events;

• travel with and visits to major gift donors, possibly in the company of more senior staff or volunteers; and

• direction of a major donor recognition project.

Some development programs expect major gift staff to secure sizable commitments from individuals without having first-hand knowledge of the prospective givers. Such an approach will never lead a major gift effort to productive solicitations. I am incredulous that development leadership could adopt such a short-sighted practice.

Today, with the large size of many organizations and the pressure to secure significant gifts, it is unfortunate that major gift work may take on an ivory-tower aspect. Instead of reaching out and encouraging many appropriate members of the community to become engaged in major gift relationships, some major gift staff create an environment of exaggerated exclusivity and inappropriate information hoarding. Nothing is more harmful and counter-productive to the institutional climate for fund raising than elitist behavior by development staff.

Constituency knowledge. Although coming at the end of this triad, learning about and gaining insight into the personalities and motivations of possible significant givers is the *raison d'etre* of the major gift staff person. While files, biographical sketches, trip reports, memo, and newspaper clippings are helpful, two sources of information are far superior: knowledge gained directly from the prospective giver or from those who know the giver well. Thus, the major gift officer must work to get as "close to the customer" as possible.

Several years ago our firm did a study on staff retention that indicated that one key factor to keeping staff was to offer them training opportunities. Staff felt valued when supervisors and colleagues invested in their growth. Thus, in a field such as major gifts where the continuity of relationships is vital, training is an exceptional investment.

Running the gamut from tracking systems to structuring deferred gifts, there is virtually no limit to what major gift officers can learn by attending professional conferences, such as those sponsored by CASE, or by visiting colleagues in well-respected programs. However, please don't ignore that some of the best teachers are right in your midst—within the development office, on your board, in volunteer groups, and on the faculty in such areas as motivational psychology.

Supervising and evaluating major gift staff

Because the results of major gift programs are both impressive and vital, there is a tendency to measure them primarily by quantitative indicators. However, major gift work is the consummate donor-focused, team-building program; and, therefore, qualitative indicators are equally important.

In the name of productivity, I occasionally see well-meaning supervisors who have arrayed the names of all the major gift prospects, their gift rating, and a staff name on a chart. This graphic display can perpetuate the misunderstanding that "major gift staff member X is responsible for raising $3 million this year." Rather, major gift staff member X is responsible for managing the relationships with a group of major gift prospects who, if properly informed, involved, and solicited, may commit $3 million.

This distinction is not at odds with a quantitative major gift model such as the one proposed by Don Myers in Chapter 4. In that model a staff member would normally have an annual goal of raising $625,000. It is important to note, however, that the goal is negotiated by the major gift officer and his or her supervisor based on the number of prospects who are at a stage in their relationship where asking for a gift is appropriate. Moreover, the solicitation of these prospects is only one of the major gift officer's overall responsibilities in advancing the relationships of a much larger pool of prospective donors.

Therefore, what we really want to evaluate is *how the staff person manages relationships.* "X" should be able to:

- identify prospective major givers;
- discover or create friendships and activities that will draw givers into the life of the institution;
- determine the philanthropic interests and motivations of donors; and
- assist volunteers, the president or head, or the chief development officer in approaching donors for major commitments.

Is "X" sensitive to the friendships and communications that provide both the stimulation and the leverage to foster significant giving? This is the donor-focused aspect of the major gift role.

The team-building skills of the major gift officer can be evaluated in his or her support of volunteers, faculty, or staff who interact with the major giver. And, since major gift programs also benefit from the work done in annual funds, planned giving, and alumni affairs, the major gift staff person should also be measured on how well he or she utilizes the talents of the full institutional advancement team.

To communicate to the many players involved with major gift prospects, the staff person should oversee a tracking system that provides timely updates on the plan, status, and next steps for each giver. Also, the major gift staff person urges and prods those with key relationships to major givers to stay in touch with them— by drafting correspondence, setting up visits, and generally being good stewards.

Supervision of a major gift program requires weekly meetings to review the status of the prospects, determine next steps, and share information. Occasionally you may be tempted to replace meetings with periodic memoranda or computer printouts. Such a practice usually produces quite an exchange of paper and no interpersonal contact, either among staff or with donors. Thus, you must fight the urge to over-regulate or minimize the personal involvement of a large number of people in the major gift program. In their best form, successful major gift programs are really tribal societies, with the more junior members sitting around the table, hearing "war stories," and learning from their professional "elders."

Conclusion

One of the lessons the junior development officers will learn from these "elders" is that they are not expected to be supermen or superwomen. Useful though superhuman speed and the ability to leap over huge bureaucratic obstacles might be, they are not prerequisites for success. What is required for success is a fundamental integrity, a willingness to listen, and a commitment to the institution and its mission.

Chapter 4

Setting Guidelines: Assessing And Directing Major Gift Staff For Optimal Results

Don Myers
Assistant Vice President and Director of Development
University of Georgia
Athens, Georgia
(Formerly Assistant Dean for Development and Alumni Relations,
University of Pennsylvania)

To sustain an effective and efficient major gift program, staff members must focus their time and energy on the central mission of major gift fund raising—building relationships between the institution and its prospects. Though this seems a simple, forthright goal, it can be a difficult one to achieve. How much time should a major gift officer devote to establishing and nurturing a single prospect relationship? How can officers determine whether or not they are using their time and energy efficiently? How many prospects should staff contact during the year? How many successful solicitations, and at what gift level, can the director of a major gift program expect an officer to achieve?

To answer these questions and address other major gift staff management issues, the University of Pennsylvania (Penn) designed a set of guidelines by which to manage its major gift staff better. The guidelines set forth management objectives and goals by:

- defining the scope and nature of each officer's workload;
- determining the amount and quality of interactions that major gift staff should pursue with prospects;
- establishing how many successful solicitations each officer should achieve in a given period; and

25

• determining how much financial support each officer should set as a goal for achievement.

The guidelines outline the work and goals of each major gift officer for the period of one year. Moreover, the guidelines give the entire major gift program a "benchmark" by which to measure its overall success and efficiency.

Though Penn developed these guidelines for its own program, you may adapt or modify them for use in your own major gift enterprise. In adapting this model, however, keep the purpose of the guidelines firmly in mind—namely, to advance meaningful relationships with prospects that result in increased support. Avoid using the guidelines to set artificial, quantifiable goals based on what your institution might like to achieve. Rather, use the guidelines to build and track the prospect/institution relationship. Though the guidelines set yearly goals, the focus of your major gift management program must remain on the long-term process of building prospect relationships.

Using the guidelines to determine the nature and scope of work

Each major gift officer occupies a different level of staffing, is responsible for specific management objectives, and works with a unique pool of prospects. The guidelines weigh these factors for each major gift officer, and provide a profile of each officer's workload. Armed with this profile, the manager and the major gift officer have a background for discussing current and future work. The profile also provides a basis for measuring the performance and success of the major gift officer.

Defining work profiles. Establishing the work profiles is the first step in negotiating the parameters of the guidelines. To define and measure the work profiles, the manager and major gift officer assess how much time the officer devotes to each area of his or her fund-raising responsibilities. Besides an officer's major gift responsibilities, he or she may work in other areas such as:
• management and direction of other staff;
• annual giving tasks;
• alumni affairs and communications; and
• admissions activities.

Understanding all the ingredients. Knowing the specific percentage of time that staff devotes to major gift activities is not enough; it is also important that managers and staff understand the nature of specific major gift work. Several factors contribute to the ease or difficulty of a major gift officer's work. Before you determine quantitative goals, it is important that you understand how these factors shape each officer's work:

Volunteer management. Volunteers can aid the officers by "moving" key prospects. However, cultivating and managing volunteers takes time away from an officer's ability to close major gifts. If an officer is responsible for intensive volunteer organizing, this officer may not be able to close as many gifts as an officer who has few volunteer responsibilities.

Administrative vs. development duties. Most major gift officers have non-development responsibilities to the dean, directors, or other administrators. Though this work is essential to coordinating the administrative and the development roles of your institution, it can take major gift officers away from fund-raising duties. It is critical that officers and managers "keep their balance" when dividing their energies between administrative and development duties.

Faculty interaction and support. Some development officers assist faculty in finding and pursuing funding for faculty projects and research. Institutions may even assign development officers to aid these faculty members. While these are logical obligations, they can draw major gift officers away from fulfilling their responsibilities to the major gift program.

Nature of the officer's prospect pool. Several elements define a given officer's prospect pool and his or her ability to deal with these prospects:

1. Location of the prospects. If all the prospects in an officer's pool live in one metropolitan area, they are more accessible than if they are located in several states or spread across the nation. In addition, when prospects live close to the institution, they tend to feel more connected to the institution. This connection can make prospects more open to initial cultivation by the officer.

2. Prospects' ability to give. Common sense tells us that prospects who have the ability to give a major gift also offer the greatest potential for fund-raising success. Therefore, an officer hopes to have as many "able" prospects in his or her pool as possible. A prospect pool peopled with these donors allows the officer to eliminate from his or her pool prospects with poor inclination levels. In addition, such prospects usually put the major gift officer in contact with other, like-minded donors.

3. Prospects' inclination to give. Behind ability, inclination to give is an essential ingredient for turning a prospect into a major gift donor. If your institution is a high-giving priority for a prospect, he or she will have a greater inclination to give a major gift. Therefore, officers strive to identify and cultivate as many "inclined" prospects within their prospect pool as possible.

4. Fund-raising experience of the officer. In general, the more fund-raising experience a major gift officer possesses, the more efficient and effective that officer will be in handling the major gift process. Related, the degree to which a major gift officer knows his or her institution will affect his or her fund-raising effectiveness. Officers who know their institution inside and out can relay information regarding the institution to prospects confidently and expertly.

5. Officers' access to administrative support and resources. Do your major gift officers do their own clerical work, writing, and research? Is their access to office equipment and computer resources limited? When officers have little administrative support, or must work with poor equipment and inadequate research resources, they will have less time to close major gifts.

6. Officers' access to operational funds. Balancing the prudent use of an operating budget with the needs of staff members is key to the efficiency of any development program. When there are few constraints on the major gift operating budget, officers can maintain contact with prospects more easily and effectively. It is important that officers have adequate access to the funds they need to visit and cultivate prospects.

7. Officers' involvement in campaigns. When major gift officers cultivate prospects through a campaign, it is important to understand where the campaign is in its timeline. The duties of the major gift officer will change with the particular stages of the campaign. Each of these stages requires that the officer devote varying amounts of work, as well as take up different roles.

During the *pre-campaign stage*, the officer is concerned with researching and identifying prospects. The officer creates needs lists for the campaign and strategies for cultivating particular prospects. During the *nucleus fund stage*, the officer concentrates on securing lead gifts from trustees, alumni, and other prospects with the greatest giving capacity. The *full campaign stage* marks the time when the campaign is fully in progress. At this time the officer focuses on solicitation activities.

The *post-campaign stage* refers to the period immediately after the campaign's end. During this time, the officer lays the groundwork for stewardship with the campaign's donors. This work is critical for helping donors, particularly alumni, maintain their connection and involvement with the institution.

Establishing quantifiable goals

After you have determined the nature and scope of each officer's work, you are ready to set the quantifiable goals of the guidelines. These goals include the number of contacts, or "moves," an officer should expect to make with prospects. In addition, the goals should give each officer a benchmark for the amount of support he or she should raise for the institution.

Making the "moves"

The guidelines propose that each major gift officer make a specific number of meaningful moves with major gift prospects. Each move is an actual step in the major gift process. Before the officers begin to make or document their moves, they divide the total prospect pool among themselves. This practice provides each officer with a defined prospect pool and eliminates the possible overlap of efforts.

Because direct contact is the most effective way of cultivating, soliciting, and thanking donors, the majority of these moves are face-to-face contacts. In some circumstances, officers may find that it is best to make contact with prospects by telephone or letter. Each prospect has different needs, preferences, and his or her own privacy boundaries. Major gift officers should call on their own expertise and knowledge of the prospect to determine the most effective means of communication with a prospect.

Officers document each of their moves within the tracking system. In addition, officers maintain a running total of the number of visits made, the number of gifts made, the amount of money raised, and the amount of money soon to be raised.

During progress report meetings, officers review this data with their manager. To avoid postponing top priority moves or missing opportunities, the manager tracks the moves of each major gift officer closely.

Understanding the various types of moves. Moves can be broken down into clear categories. It is important that officers and managers understand the types of moves in order to track their work effectively.

Early cultivation moves. Through this type of move officers isolate a list of prospects for cultivation. Usually, research staff members have targeted these prospects as individuals who have the capacity and inclination to give a major gift. The officer then visits these prospects to define their capacity and inclination to give more clearly and to encourage the growth of a giving relationship.

Cultivation moves. After early cultivation has determined that a prospect has the capacity and inclination to give, the officer begins cultivation moves. During cultivation moves, major gift officers visit prospects to explain the funding needs of the institution. The officer may describe specific project needs as well as general needs. Ideally, the officer frames giving opportunities in a away that fit the desires, beliefs, and convictions of the prospect. The major gift officer should ask the prospect for his or her opinions on the project and be prepared to talk intelligently about projects that may be of interest to the prospect. Moreover, cultivation moves should strengthen the prospect's inclination toward the institution.

Solicitation moves. An officer undertakes solicitation moves when he or she has determined that a prospect is ready and willing to provide support to the institution. During these moves, the major gift officer asks for a specific gift. Usually, this gift is one for which the prospect showed interest during the cultivation stage. The officer should offer the prospect a giving opportunity that both fits the needs of the prospect and the funding goals of the institution.

Stewardship moves. After a prospect has provided a major gift to the institution, he or she becomes a donor. Through stewardship moves, the officer ensures that the institution expresses its special thanks and appreciation to donors. Successful stewardship moves should also keep donors engaged and involved with the institution. Officers should update prospects regularly regarding how their gifts are benefitting the institution or a project. Stewardship includes inviting donors to fund-raising events, especially events that honor the project a donor has funded. Thorough stewardship keeps donors current with the life of the institution, its triumphs, and its emerging needs.

Using Penn's guidelines as a model

Penn's guidelines define major gift prospects as those individuals with the ability and inclination to provide a $25,000 gift. Penn's guidelines direct each major gift officer to make 200 moves with prospects per year. To meet this goal, major gift officers plan five to six moves per week for approximately 40 weeks of the 52-week year.

Penn's guidelines show that the major gift activities of its officers have a specific composition. Their moves break down as:
- 25 percent early cultivation moves;
- 25 percent cultivation moves;
- 30 percent solicitation moves; and
- 20 percent stewardship moves.

Achieving support goals. Each officer strives to achieve an annual support goal of closing 25 major gifts. These gifts should total a minimum of $625,000. Ideally, this total should reflect the closure of 25 gifts at the $25,000 level. Although it is unlikely that the institution will receive 25 gifts at exactly $25,000, the "25/25 rule" gives officers a tangible goal to pursue. In reality, the larger gifts will balance the smaller gifts to reach the $625,000 goal.

A typical major gift portfolio. Each major gift officer manages a portfolio of 150 active prospects drawn from the total pool of $25,000 and above prospects. This portfolio divides the officer's prospect pool into categories that reflect the progress of the relationship-building process. For example, 50 prospects may be within 12 months of closure while 100 prospects may be further away from closure.

The portfolio cross-lists prospects by their geographic region and according to their giving capacity and inclination ratings. This enables the officers to schedule visits around the "best" prospects within a particular geographic region.

Seeking new prospects from existing ones. While meeting with donors, major gift officers ask them to suggest other prospects who may have an interest in the institution. The officers strive to identify 50 new prospects annually. Research staff then review these new prospects for early cultivation, and the relationship-building cycle begins anew.

During the year, each major gift officer continually makes moves, updates his or her portfolio of active prospects, identifies new prospects, and closes major gifts. Each of these tasks is the officer's responsibility, and one task is not forsaken for another.

Conclusion

These guidelines are an excellent starting point for handling the myriad challenges that managing a major gift program entails. The guidelines provide an opportunity for managers and major gift officers to work together to determine the most effective use of the officers' time. Moreover, these guidelines give major gift officers a foundation on which to base and measure the success of their efforts. The guidelines allow officers to devote their attention and skill to the primary work of a major gift program—building relationships that will lead to greater private support for the institution.

Chapter 5

Prospect Research: Key Methods for Discovering And Targeting Donors

John Gliha
Consultant
Marts and Lundy, Inc.
Lyndhurst, New Jersey

Nurturing donor relationships, managing development staff, and conducting donor events are all activities that, when executed effectively, will take your major donor program far down the road to the proverbial "pot of major gift gold." These activities are most easily conducted with alumni of your institution or other individuals who are directly involved with the life of your institution. But how does your institution find major donors who do not fit into either one of these categories? How do you find prospects who may have the ability and inclination to give to your organization, but only need to be cultivated as donors? How do you research the financial assets and philanthropic interests of these prospects? How do you find out more about prospects who are already generally known to your institution, but about whom you would like to have more than sketchy information? And finally, are there any moral or legal guidelines to which you should adhere when conducting such research?

Thorough, honest prospect research can answer many of these basic questions. This chapter will help the newcomer to prospect research understand:
- the purpose and goals of prospect research;
- how to conduct appropriate prospect research;
- how to use public sources;
- how to combine research with institutional memory; and
- how to protect your institution and prospects from right of privacy invasions.

Seasoned researchers will find this chapter useful as a refresher to "point up" improvements for existing prospect research operations. The "Prospect Research Bibliography" at the end of this book provides basic, up-to-date sources for conducting thorough prospect research, both for the novice and the experienced researcher.

Where does prospect research fit into the development matrix?

Institutional advancement officers have conducted prospect research to target and qualify potential major donors for many years. During the past decade, however, the field of prospect research has experienced unprecedented growth and development. Part of this growth is attributable to the increasing need for institutions to expand their support base. Much of prospect research's growth, however, is a direct result of the technological advancements that faster and more efficient computers have brought to the processing of information. Information that was once burdensome and time-consuming to gather is now available in seconds or minutes. A few keystrokes on an on-line database can provide information that, in the past, would have required making several phone calls or composing letters of request. Rather than visiting record offices and libraries, prospect researchers can "call up" information on computers no further away that their desks.

Indeed, today's prospect research capabilities testify that the "information age" has come to fund raising. As research technologies have improved, development programs have demanded and relied upon the more in-depth information that is available to them. As a result, prospect research plays an increasingly important role in the development process. Prospect research has become an integral aspect of any successful development operation.

Balancing privacy rights with the need for information

While the expansion of available information gives the researcher more choices in conducting research, it doesn't necessarily make his or her job any easier. With all that is available at the researcher's fingertips, what is appropriate information to gather on a single prospect? How can the researcher find out enough about a prospect to begin cultivation without infringing on that prospect's privacy?

Today's researchers are researching and retrieving the same types of donor information that has always existed within the public domain. Prior to the "computer age" this information was protected by its sheer bulkiness; because paper documents were the only means of recording documents, much information was protected de facto through the physical constraints involved in its retrieval. In today's fast-paced, electronic data-driven society, however, researchers can transfer over great distances information that once rested securely in a manilla file folder. Moreover, computer on-line services allow researchers to retrieve, compile, and analyze information for minimal expense and effort.

Right of privacy. Since its founding, the United States has based the legal, personal rights of its citizens upon the principle of the "right of privacy." The right of privacy is roughly defined as the right of individuals to determine the type and extent to which information about themselves may be disclosed to others. In recent years, this right has become particularly vulnerable with the development of increasingly sophisticated electronic methods for storing, retrieving, and communicating information.

In 1965, the U.S. Supreme Court formally recognized that an individual has a constitutional right of privacy. The Court based this right of privacy doctrine upon the Bill of Right's guarantees of free speech and association, freedom from unreasonable searches and seizures, the right to remain silent, and the unenumerated Ninth Amendment rights "retained by the people." [*Griswold v. Connecticut*, 381 U.S. 479 (1965)]. This decision, other legal precedent, and the founding principles of our nation have sewn the right of privacy doctrine into the fabric of our legal, ethical, and business practices.

Protecting the prospect's right of privacy. Prospect research can bring affluent, generous donors to the doors of your institution; it can also invade the privacy of these donors, alienating them (and other donors) from your institution. Indeed, prospect researchers possess a staggering ability to delve into the lives of individuals. If this ability is misused or misdirected, the consequences to your institutions can be disastrous. At every step of the research process, prospect researchers must balance a prospect's right of privacy against institutional rights and needs.

Conducting nonintrusive research

Three elements should be considered when collecting information which may intrude upon a prospect's right of privacy.

First, is **relevance**. Researchers should limit their inquiries regarding a prospect's affairs to those areas that are directly relevant to the informational needs at hand. Limit the collection of peripheral information. For example, although a researcher may review divorce records, it may be inappropriate to delve into the specific reasons leading to the separation. The task of the researcher is to ascertain the financial distribution of the marital assets, not the personal character of the individual. As a general rule, researchers should treat all collected information as being highly personal and sensitive, and as such, confidential in nature.

Second, **honesty** should mark the conduct of researchers and their search methodologies. Research staff must be forthright about the collection of information. They should not use false names or pretenses as justification for gathering data. Research staff must be able to distinguish investigative methods that are ordinary and reasonable from those which are neither. Moreover, researchers must constantly evaluate their methods from a privacy perspective, and adjust their practices accordingly.

The third consideration is **consent**. Is the prospect likely to consent to the sort of inquiry that you are conducting? Because prospect research is, by its very nature, a personal investigation, researchers must ensure that their practices do not trample the personal consent of any donor. When research methods ignore consent, they can alienate prospective donors — an outcome that is tantamount to throwing out the baby with the bath water.

The issue of consent directly affects the relationship between the institution and the prospect. Since most states have enacted disclosure requirements for records related to individuals, prospects may ask to review their own research files. If the research process has followed the reasonable and respectable guidelines, this eventuality should pose no threat. However, if a prospect's file maintains derogatory speculation or inaccurate, unnecessary, or unsubstantiated information, such conduct could jeopardize the institution's ongoing relationship with the prospect.

In 1991, CASE's Educational Fund Raising Commission published *Principles and Recommendations Regarding Ethics and Confidentiality in Development Research* to help researchers and other development professionals balance privacy considerations with fund-raising needs. Developed from two years of discussion with a wide range of advancement professionals, these guidelines provide basic principles and recommendations regarding ethics and confidentiality in development research. In addition to reviewing these principles, your institution may also want to develop internal policies regarding prospect research and information management.

Elements of research

Giving is a personal decision, based upon the complexities of each donor's character and personality. Although many ingredients combine to cause any donor to give, three major factors influence the prospect's decision to make a large gift to an institution. First, and most important, is the prospect's *giving capacity*. Second, is the prospect's *relationship to the institution* and the cause at hand. Third, is the prospect's *relationship with the solicitor*, preferably a peer volunteer. Each of these elements is an important element for analysis and inclusion in the research report.

Organizing and narrowing the scope of your research

Before you can analyze prospects according to these three elements, you must decide which prospects you will include in your research. In other words, you must narrow the scope of your research to a manageable and logical set of prospects. Your institution may already possess a list of prospects who are believed to have significant giving potential. Your first task as a researcher is to reduce this large list of prospects to a smaller, targeted group that can be researched more fully.

At this initial level of research, the prospect researcher should conduct basic, screening research. This task entails researching the list of prospects using a defined set of readily available reference sources. The initial reference needs of each institution will be different, and will depend on its support constituency and the focus of its fund raising. Some resources that are useful for initial research include:
- *Standard and Poor's Register*;
- *Marquis Who's Who* Index;
- *Who's Wealthy in America*;

- *Dun's Reference Book of Corporate Management;*
- CDA Invest/Net;
- *Forbes* "400 List"; and
- internal alumni records.

The main purpose of this initial research is to determine whether or not the individual has the "meat and mettle" of major gift prospect, thus justifying more in-depth research. Initial screening should also provide major gift officers with information about the prospect that will make initial contact with the prospect meaningful and engaging.

Assessing the prospect's capacity to give

After you have screened your pool of prospects and determined a list to be researched, you may begin real individual assessments. Though you may begin your research by investigating any of the three basic elements, it is a good idea to begin with the "nuts and bolts" element — the prospect's capacity to give. Donors lacking this capacity may be of enormous help to your institution, however only donors with adequate capacity to give will ever be able to offer major gift support.

Several clues indicate a prospect's capacity to give. Some indicators are straightforward; a certain level of salary leaves little doubt of a prospect's capacity to give. Other indicators, such as stock holdings, inheritance wealth, and real estate investments, are key points of reference for assessing a prospect's wealth. As a researcher, you should not limit your assessment to a single indicator. Only when you combine all aspects of a prospect's wealth, will you get a clear sense of that prospect's potential as a major donor.

Salary. In many instances, salary information is the single most important element in assessing a prospect's giving capacity. Even when this is not the case, salary will almost always be a major consideration in your prospect research.

Salaries of upper-level corporate officers of publicly traded companies can usually be found in the proxy statement. A proxy statement announces the annual meeting of publicly held companies and contains extensive financial information about corporate management. For example, it reports the salaries, contingent renumeration, and benefits for top corporate executives. The proxy statement will also reveal the stock holdings of the company directors, as well as any non-director five percent stock holders. The proxy statement usually contains brief biographies of the directors, which detail their other directorships, history with the company, and volunteer and philanthropic interests.

The salaries of government employees are always publicly available through the respective government agencies for which they work. (The Freedom of Information Act guarantees access to government salary information). To learn about a specific salary, call the appropriate agency to determine the procedure for requesting salary records.

To determine an estimate of the salary income for an individual, you may want consult the *American Almanac of Jobs and Salaries*. This reference tool lists salaries and other forms of compensation for individuals by profession or employment. In addition, the *Almanac* tracks salary differences for different professions according to the region of the country in which the prospect works.

Sometimes, you may be unable to ascertain an estimated salary level through any of these means. To solve this problem, many researchers develop their own in-house database, which records relationships between known salaries, job titles, regional location, and company size. This type of analytical data collection can also be a helpful tool for estimating probable salary and income.

Salary bonuses. Salary alone may not always make up the largest portion of an individual's yearly income. Many prospects may receive substantial salary bonuses as part of their income compensation package. Bonuses for most company employees are often difficult to determine. For major corporate officers, however, details of bonuses can be found in the proxy statement.

Stock investments. Stocks and stock options may contribute significantly to a donor's assets. Therefore, research into this area of a prospect's assets may be invaluable to estimating that prospect's giving capability.

The alert researcher should evaluate the prospect's stock portfolio from several aspects. In particular, research should determine significant capital gains or losses in the prospect's activities. Sustained gains may enable the prospect to consider making a large charitable gift, while easing income tax burdens. Substantial losses may discourage the donor's inclination to make a substantial charitable gift.

Several public sources will reveal important information necessary to evaluating a prospect's stock portfolio. The Securities Act of 1934 established filing requirements for all individuals who are "inside owners" or five percent owners of publicly traded companies. This information is available within the proxy statements of public companies.

Researchers should also take dividend earnings from stock ownership into account when reviewing stock portfolios. The *Wall Street Journal* and all major newspapers publish the amount of annual dividends that companies pay to stock holders; this amount is recorded immediately after the company symbol. To determine annual earnings from stock dividends, simply multiply the dividend amount by the number of shares owned by the prospect.

Another information source on stock holdings for insiders and five percent holders is the on-line service offered by the Invest/Net Group. Developed for use by the Securities and Exchange Commission, this database lists each insider's total "direct" and "indirect" stock ownership for the companies with which they are associated. The Invest/Net on-line service lists the purchase and sale price for each block of stock traded by the insider. The service even indicates if that individual has transferred shares of stock as a gift. By comparing the purchase price and current trading price of the blocks of stock, the researcher can ascertain capital gains or losses. Users can search the database by the prospect's name.

Business and corporate investments. The financial status of a company or foundation that a prospect controls may reflect the personal wealth of that prospect. To investigate such wealth, you should obtain the annual reports on the corporations of interest. Annual reports usually contain such information as: the corporation's formal business name; a listing of officers, directors, and five percent stock holders; the nature and practices of the business enterprise; and a summary balance sheet of assets and liabilities.

In most states, both public and privately held companies must file annual reports with the appropriate state agency. The reporting structure and titles for these offices vary by state, but usually companies must file with the incorporating division of the Secretary of State's Office. For example, the Arizona Corporation

Commission holds the annual filings for any company or foundation operating in the state of Arizona. Through these offices, you may purchase annual reports of companies for a nominal fee. Foundations offer their annual reports for free with a request over the phone or in writing.

Retirement benefits. In today's career market, more than salary and bonuses make up the total compensation package of many employees. Retirement benefits can constitute a significant portion of an individual's future assets. This is especially true for upper management employees and high-ranking corporate officers. Therefore, it is a good idea to research the real and estimated retirement benefits for these individuals.

To research the retirement benefits for major corporate officers you need only consult the proxy statement for that corporation. The corporation's proxy statement publishes the retirement benefits of corporate officers. However, the exact retirement benefits of other corporate employees are not available in the proxy statement. To learn the retirement benefits of these individuals, you will need to derive estimated retirement benefits. To determine such estimates, try reviewing the corporation's executive recruitment packets. These documents will often list the retirement plans and benefits that the company provides as part of its employment packages. From this information, you can extrapolate an estimated retirement benefit for the prospect.

Real estate investments. Property value is also an important factor in figuring out an individual's philanthropic capability. The easiest way to approximate the worth of a person's home or other property is through the local Assessor's Office.

At the County Assessor's Office, you will want to review the deed to the prospect's home. Remember that the prospect may own the property in a name other than his or her own or through another related entity. Besides owning property in his or her own name, an individual may list property in the name of his or her company, through a real estate trust, or in the name of a spouse or close family member. In addition, you may find it helpful to review deeds to income properties, such as rental property. The information you glean regarding income properties will give added insight into the income of the prospect.

When searching property records, you should obtain:

- the assessed value of the property;
- the date of the assessment;
- the percent of the market value of the assessment; and
- a description of the property, including any improvements that have been made to it.

Other sources can help you establish approximate property values. Most local newspapers or real estate guides publish the sale price of homes and properties. In regions serviced by small regional papers, this information may be harder to come by. Some on-line services, such as DataTimes, index the real estate sale prices published in smaller regional news sources.

Several publications record the history and prices of real estate conveyances. For example, the *Lusk Report*, a Washington, DC, regional publication, lists every home in the District, when it was built, when it was last sold, the amount of the sale, the name(s) of the present owners, and the value of the current assessment. Thus, even if the prospect has been living in the same house for the last 25 years, you can still find the most recent sale values of a house in his or her neighborhood. To find similar publications for your locality, check *Gale's Directory of Publica-*

tions. It may also be helpful to contact a local real estate agent to recommend services that can provide this information.

Inheritances. Although inheritance wealth does not reflect current assets, it is an important aspect of a prospect's total wealth. Obviously, information on an individual's inheritance wealth tells you how much this prospect stands to gain in the future. However, the information that you gather may also tell you how a prospect is currently managing his or her money against the day that an inheritance becomes real. Substantial inheritance wealth may flag a family's future need to defray inheritance tax burdens through a planned gift. Though inheritance information may seem mutable, it can give the researcher an important view into a prospect's lifetime financial strategy.

Given that inheritance wealth is an intimate subject for most individuals, how does the researcher gain access to such information? Readily available print resources are not always helpful for investigating inherited family wealth. Therefore, you may have to undertake some aboveboard, but understated "sleuth work" to learn more about an individual's inheritance wealth.

Begin your investigation by inspecting the wills of closely related family members, including the parents of both the prospect and his or her spouse. Once a will is in probate, it is in the public domain and is available for reading at the courthouse in which it was processed.

When reading a probated will, you should be certain to review several specific items. Foremost, be sure to read the division of the estate in detail. This will give you an idea of how the will disburses and manages the estate. For example, the division of the estate will show whether the wealth of the estate will be meted out in direct inheritances or disbursed over time through trusts.

When reviewing a will, you should also familiarize yourself with the inventory of the estate. This document will list all securities belonging to the decedent, cash on hand, an appraisal of personal property (usually furniture and jewelry), and real estate holdings.

If the will does not include an inventory of the estate, consult the estate tax bill from either the state or the IRS. These bills are based upon a formula that can help you determine the size of the taxable estate, as the tax value reflects a specific fraction of the real value of the estate. To figure the worth of the taxable estate, obtain tax tables directly from the IRS or the appropriate state of residence. Then calculate the total estate value from the current tax formulas.

In addition, the will should include a complete list of relatives receiving inheritances from the estate. If the estate is particularly large, you might wish to review the inheritance structure of the will to find out how the family will manage its wealth in the future. This list can also reveal relatives and relationships that may be of interest to your development effort.

Other investment considerations. One of the most difficult factors in assessing the financial capability of a prospect is discovering his or her liabilities. These can range from the obvious to the obscure. Some prospects may devote substantial financial commitments to family members. They may have children at home or in college, or they may support an elderly parent. Other prospects may spend much of their income to maintain a specific lifestyle. These prospects may own expensive cars, boats, or planes. They may enjoy expensive hobbies, such as the collection of art or antiques.

Liability factors provide useful benchmarks in establishing a prospect's total financial profile. However, information on liability can also help your institution's cultivation efforts. Such research may reveal a special funding interest of the donor that was previously unknown. Moreover, this sort of detailed information may flag prospects that can offer gifts in kind.

Researching the prospect's relationship with your institution

Once you have determined that the prospect has the financial capability to make a major gift, you may proceed to the next order of prospect research business—defining the prospect's relationship to your institution. To do this, you will review in-house tracking records, prospect records, and call on the knowledge of staff and volunteers. You may also survey the prospects themselves for a true "insider" view of their ties to your institution

Elements to look for. As a researcher, you must learn as much as possible about the prospect's past relationship with the institution. Your research should answer such questions as:

1. Is the prospect an alumnus, alumna, parent, or friend?
2. Has the prospect been a donor in the past?
3. To what programs or departments has the prospect made gifts?
4. What were the amounts of these gifts?
5. Have other family members of the prospect attended or been involved with the institution?

Where past gifts indicate the "quantity" of the prospect's relationship with your institution, personal involvement measures the "quality" of this relationship. As the prospect researcher, you should try to get a feel for the quality of each prospect's relationship with your institution. Look for a history of volunteer involvement, such as service on advisory boards or councils. For prospects who have not involved themselves directly with your institution, keep an eye out for volunteer service to nonprofit organizations, charities, and other social causes.

It is also important to identify any problems that the prospect or his or her family may have had with your institution. Has the matriarch of the prospect's family publicly refused to give to any institutions of your kind? If so, you should caution solicitation staff to tread carefully when taking their first cultivation steps with that prospect.

Locating prospect relationship information. As a prospect researcher, your best source of information will exist in your "institutional memory." This includes hard-copy and computerized records relating to the prospect, such as tracking records, solicitors' notes, volunteer histories, and other institutional documents. Institutional memory also includes the information that staff have "in their heads." Although their reflections may seem anecdotal in nature, development staff, key administrators, and faculty often possess important firsthand knowledge of prospects. This information may not fit into the tracking format or seem to belong in any record. Nevertheless, it can add considerable depth to a prospect's assessment.

Collecting information within your institution. Review of institutional records will be a straightforward endeavor; collecting anecdotal information may require that you employ various research techniques. You may wish to use a written survey or screening format to uncover information. Using this method, staff, administrators, and faculty review a list of prospects and indicate the prospects with whom they have a relationship. They should also describe the nature and intensity of these relationships.

After you have learned "who knows who," you should meet with these individuals to glean from them their knowledge of the prospect. These interviews often yield a great deal of helpful prospect information that the organizational records have not captured. Use caution when collecting information in this way, however. You should be careful to query and record only that information that can be substantiated or has particular relevance to your informational needs. Screening programs that encourage individuals to speculate about prospects can easily degenerate into meaningless gossip sessions.

Keep written summaries of these interviews. Written summaries will help your development team in future efforts, and provide a living institutional memory where one had not previously existed. As always, it is particularly important that privacy-based guidelines apply to any interviews for anecdotal information on prospects. Moreover, you should cull the data before committing it to the files, thereby ensuring that the records are as factual and respectful of the prospect's privacy as possible.

Collecting information from prospects. Another excellent means of collecting information relating to institutional linkages is to conduct a written survey of the prospect pool. This allows the institution to collect firsthand from prospects information relating to their physical, professional, and emotional involvement with the organization. Such surveys can yield valuable information regarding: occupational advancement and professional positions; interest in particular athletic, educational, or research programs; general attitudes toward your institution; and household income levels.

An organized and thoughtfully constructed prospect survey can yield many benefits for your prospect research effort and your institution. Such surveys provide a cost-effective and timely means of gathering data on key constituents. In addition, they can serve as an important cultivation tool. By including questions on the survey that ask about the prospect's interests within the institution, you can get a fuller picture of the prospect's philanthropic interests. Such information can be invaluable to the future cultivation of the prospect by development staff.

Researching the prospect's relationship with solicitors

To gain a clearer understanding of the prospect and his or her motivations, interests, and history with your institution, consult past solicitors for gifts. They offer an almost unparalleled source of prospect information. Because these individuals have had direct contact with the prospect, they can often offer the important details that development staff and records cannot.

Development staff and administrative officers, such as board chairpersons and the president, are obvious sources for solicitor information, as these individuals are often on the front line of the "asks." Locating past solicitors and gleaning their knowledge involves the same processes as does getting prospect information from staff, administrators, and faculty. The major gift officer of your institution should have lists of solicitors and their solicitation histories readily available. Volunteer information, such as lists of volunteers for campaigns, is also a good source for tracking down solicitors.

When interviewing solicitors, you should be especially careful to uphold the privacy guidelines of your institution. Since many volunteer solicitors are often major donors themselves, they will bring their own sensitivity to research queries that you should make every effort to respect.

Building and organizing your prospect research library

To expedite your prospect research efforts in the most economical and efficient way, it is important to build and organize a research library. Though it is not always possible, this process should move forward in a proactive, rather than a reactive, way. In other words, planned research needs, rather than "crisis" needs, should shape your research library.

Before you purchase reference resources and on-line services for your in-house prospect research library, it is important to gain an understanding of your institution's donor base. The smaller and less national your alumni and donor base, the more important it is to analyze your donor constituency prior to making in-house library decisions. Here, it may not be a good use of your research budget to build an extensive library when a smaller, targeted library might be more useful. This is especially true if you can rely on an institutional or regional library collection for more expensive resources.

Dedicate a specific portion of your annual budget for computerized resources. Though these computer costs may seem high, they often offer top benefits for the money. On-line resources usually provide a more cost-effective means for collecting data over the long run compared to traditional, hard-copy research. For example, if your research staff is spending several hours each week clipping newspaper or magazine sources, it may be more cost-effective to simply search and retrieve the same information through an on-line clipping service. These computerized services offer indexing and full text retrieval that is easy to operate, thorough, convenient, and less cumbersome than physically clipping articles.

To get a feel for the print and computerized resources available for building or improving your research library, consult the bibliography at the end of this book. The bibliography contains most of the basic and specialized tools for the prospect researcher, as well as brief explanations of specific sources.

Conclusion

With guidelines for ethics and confidentiality firmly in place, a development research effort can offer many rewards. It can help an institution to increase the size and quality of its major donor prospect pool. Within that pool, research can help identify natural constituencies for particular fund-raising priorities. And research can provide information on the unique capacity, qualities, and interests of an individual prospect. Moreover, effective prospect research will uncover information that is essential to building productive, long-term relationships between your institution and prospective donors for years to come. If it is conducted honestly and professionally, your prospect research program can provide a strong foundation for a successful major gift program.

Chapter 6

Prospect Management: Tracking And Coordinating Information

Carole W. Karsch
Director of Gift Planning and Financial Resource Development
Jewish Federation of Greater Philadelphia
Philadelphia, Pennsylvania
(Formerly Director of Capital Giving and Gift Planning
University of Pennsylvania)

As the information age advances—stepping more and more to a computerized rhythm—many things are changing, not the least of which are the words we use to describe our work. Today's workplace vocabulary reflects how important the gathering, organizing, and dispersal of information has become. Indeed, the information age has created whole new areas of goods and services—and the words to describe them. Words like "information," "data," "processing," and "hardware" have taken on meanings that, even two decades ago, would have seemed odd or altogether outlandish.

New meanings and terms can cause confusion and stir up problems for any organization, especially ones that make information gathering their business. Therefore, it makes sense, when organizing your major donor information tracking and management program, to make sure that all development staff understand some basic terms and concepts.

One such basic term is "management." A refresher of the definition of management can help you understand the goals and operational guidelines for an effective prospect tracking system. Management is defined as:

- a skilled handling of something;
- a whole system for the care and treatment of something;
- conducting or supervising something; and
- the executive function of planning, organizing, coordinating, directing, controlling, and supervising any industrial or business project or activity with responsibility for results.

By applying this definition to your major donor program, you can clarify goals, objectives, operations, and roles. For example, it is fairly straightforward that professional development officers "handle something" very important—namely, prospects. Organized prospect tracking provides a "system for the care and treatment" of prospects. Major donor officers are responsible for "planning, organizing, coordinating, directing, controlling, and supervising" prospect activities. This understanding of management implies process, planning, movement, and action that, taken together, will produce positive results for your institution.

To be successful, management must be a coordinated activity. To clarify, "coordinate" means:

- to bring into a common action, movement, or condition; and
- to regulate and combine in harmonious action.

With this definition firmly in hand, prospect managers must coordinate and agree upon a shared prospect strategy. Moreover, coordinated strategy cannot be strained or controversial. Rather, successful prospect management requires the harmonious coordination of all the "working parts" of your development enterprise. Tenets of basic trust and collegiality define the productive, successful development operation.

This chapter will describe the "nuts and bolts" of a successful prospect tracking system. As you read about the details of prospect tracking, and as you organize or create your own system, remember the basic principles that should guide, as well as drive, your work.

How does prospect tracking fit into the scheme of things?

A competent development information system establishes a base of working knowledge for development staff and their efforts. To develop support successfully, staff must have ready access to a large body of factual information on donors, foundations, corporations, and prospects. Ideally, staff can retrieve information easily from the development information system that houses this body of knowledge. Moreover, staff should be able to "leap" between information systems to retrieve and communicate information.

To manage the various cultivation and solicitation activities conducted with prospects, development staff need a complete base of biographical and financial information on prospects. Computerized prospect tracking systems have taken over this informational role, supplanting rooms of files and reams of notes and memoranda. In fact, computer and communications technology have provided major gift officers with an extraordinary resource for prospect management. Prospect information that was once burdensome and difficult to gather is now readily accessible through computer databases and on-line services.

In today's development market, prospect tracking systems are essential for providing biographical and gift data. Prospect information retrieval comes in various formats, ranging from one-page "snapshots" to detailed biographical scenarios. Managing information is a constant and ongoing process requiring skill and professionalism. Information managers do not simply enter information into a database. To preserve the value and usefulness of a tracking system, staff must update the information in a database at regular intervals. Information managers not only oil the wheels of a major donor program, they often fuel it by providing opportunities for new prospecting and solicitations.

What is the purpose of prospect tracking?

Computerized prospect tracking is the best way to keep track of what's happening with your institution's prospects. Prospect tracking systems enable development staff to evaluate and monitor the "movements" of major gift prospects and the staff who cultivate them. Moreover, tracking systems are effective coordination, planning, and communication tools for everyone involved in the prospect management process.

Overall functions. To provide staff with accessible and complete tracking records, the successful prospect tracking system:

- monitors progress;
- evaluates movements;
- assists staff in planning strategy;
- communicates information between development efforts and areas;
- provides progress reports for staff and volunteers;
- allows review of activities for reassignment; and
- houses and develops institutional memory.

Using tracking reports to "see" the prospect. Tracking systems can produce comprehensive biographical and gift records on major gift prospects. However, an effective and efficient tracking system provides a quick assessment of a major prospect's attributes and activities. This assessment includes both the current status of the prospect and the next steps that staff plan to take with the prospect. Prospect tracking is a snapshot—a picture set within a time frame and a preview of what will follow.

Maximizing staff allocation. Tracking reports show as much about what your staff is doing as they portray the movements of prospects. Development officers can use tracking data for staff evaluation, planning, identifying problems, and reporting to key administrators and leadership. Tracking reports should also describe the quality of staff contacts with prospects. By combining the quantitative and qualitative aspects of contacts, development managers can better measure staff effectiveness and productivity.

Measuring effectiveness through self-evaluation. Tracking allows staff to evaluate their own progress with assigned prospects. Through the system's calendar and tickler functions, staff can evaluate how effectively they manage their time and energy.

Recording your institution's prospect and donor history. Tracking systems also enable development officers to chart the history of relationships between the development staff and the supporters of an institution. Such a history can provide solicitors with the knowledge they need to link past solicitations with current cultivation. This is particularly valuable to new staff who often need to "get up to speed" quickly with their assigned prospect pool.

What are the "nuts and bolts" of organizing a prospect tracking system?

You may choose to house your tracking system in an integrated computer database system with multiple workstations, or you may operate all your tracking activities in a single personal computer. Smaller development operations may choose to track prospects by using card files and calendar systems. The ideal tracking system for your institution should meet your current prospect management needs and offer some room for growth. Whenever possible, your tracking system should integrate fully with the rest of your development computer systems. Smooth networking between systems will speed work and keep staff and volunteers in communication.

Tracking systems provide development officers with more efficient "back room" operations, thereby enabling them to have more time to secure maximum support for their institutions. Information storage and reporting capabilities of a tracking system help staff to manage their responsibilities and supervisors to evaluate staff effectiveness. Remember, a good computer system should be uncomplicated and easy to maintain. It is a resource or tool that should support, and not impede, efficient development operations.

Using an integrated database tracking system

Many integrated database tracking systems are available on the software market. To determine the best tracking system for your major donor needs, you should make sure that the system you choose can perform certain basic functions.

Prospect tracking functions. Robert Pallone, director of development information systems at the University of Pennsylvania, recommends that a good system should allow you to perform the following functions easily:
- add new prospect records;
- update existing prospect records;
- add new contact records;
- delete prospect and contact records (with warning prompts);
- extract information through reports;
- sort prospect records by single and multiple attributes;
- display the date of the last contact with the prospect;
- display the date of the next planned contact with the prospect;
- display a history of all contacts with the prospect;
- store comments and other textual records;
- translate codes into meaningful terms; and
- archive out-of-date contacts to a history file.

Ensuring that your system is user-friendly. If you choose an integrated database system, it should provide all users with simultaneous access to information. An integrated system should enable users to build a community "notebook" for sharing prospect contact information. This capability will eliminate running from office to office or waiting for weekly reports. A well-integrated system allows staff to call up prospect records and sort reports quickly and easily.

Ideally, all users should have their own computer terminals from which they may enter information directly into the system. You may also choose to limit data entry capability to a particular, trained staff person. In this case, development officers must submit information for central entry in an organized format. Figure 6-1 on page 52 is an example of a data entry form that staff can use to communicate this information to the data entry person in your office.

System capabilities. A good tracking system answers the *what-when-who* questions related to prospect activity. To answer these questions, the system should present, in a streamlined fashion, a description of past activity, current initiatives, and next steps for individual major prospects. It should also be able to sort recorded information by various attributes. These sorted batches of information should create reports that are useful to both staff and volunteers.

Tracking Components. To store information most efficiently, tracking systems store information in specific categories or "fields." In the case of prospect tracking, these fields represent the critical attributes of prospects. When creating reports, staff select the single or multiple attributes for batching into specialized reports. The key categories of information for a simple tracking system include:

- name;
- address;
- giving capability and inclination ratings;
- areas of interest;
- gift target and purpose;
- giving status of the prospect;
- solicitor(s) of the prospect;
- other staff relationships;
- date of staff assignment to the prospect;
- date of last staff or volunteer contact with the prospect;
- brief review of contact;
- nature of proposed next action; and
- date of next action.

A more complex system might add:

- primary and secondary contacts;
- date of staff reassignment;
- status of any proposals submitted to prospect; and
- status of stewardship activities with prospect (now a donor).

Using tracking reports. Individual tracking reports can be simple one-page overviews or multi-page profiles with separate entry screens for summary, status, and contacts. Master reports might include complete listings sorted alphabetically, prospect summaries, "next action" tickler project profiles, project summaries, and moves summaries. The system should be able to sort information by any of the tracking attributes, either alone or in combination. Figure 6-2 on page 53 is an example of a prospect report.

Words from the "tracking system wise." Tracking produces quick, useful information to plot the movement of major prospects through the evaluation-cultivation-solicitation-stewardship cycle. However, maintaining the system and producing tracking reports should not become an end in itself. Staff must avoid the tendency to embroil themselves in computer tasks, such as staying in the office to enter information or detail prospect relationships in cumbersome detail. The tracking system is a means, not an end.

Tracking does not replace the nuance and detail of in-depth file reports of prospect activity. Nor does tracking supplant gift strategization. Rather, tracking is a resource that allows development staff to effectively and efficiently manage the individual major gift process.

Conversely, even a perfectly planned system has limited use if staff elect to bypass it. To be truly effective, a tracking system should attract the use and attention of staff.

Prospect tracking without large databases

The focus of our discussion has been on computer-based tracking systems. Such systems are, as we have seen, efficient and effective ways to manage large numbers of prospects. With a small prospect pool or a small development staff, it is sometimes more prudent to use other prospect tracking systems.

Using card files. A card file is one approach to managing a small prospect pool. This system is the least expensive and most portable of tracking systems. Using a standard format, staff develop individual prospect cards that contain all the information development officers need for current prospect activities. As the prospect relationship moves through the various stages of the prospect management process, staff update the cards. Card files afford solicitors the opportunity to review their assigned prospect pool continuously. In addition, card files are portable and allow staff to "carry their knowledge with them."

Using personal computers (PCs). Many computer prospect management software packages run well on personal computers. If you manage a smaller development operation, you may find that a PC system is an economical answer to your tracking needs. With expert technical assistance, you can tailor a software package to make your own tracking system. If you shy away from packaged systems, you may wish to build a tracking system by augmenting your current database. Many creative information managers have done this by specializing a file manager or reorganizing a relational database.

Prospect tracking offers several other ways to track prospect information. Some development officers track prospect information on PCs by combining individual files with a running list of current prospects. Others prefer using a tickler file or calendar note reminders in concert with a hard-copy prospect list. You may wish to develop a single-page prospect tracking format that staff can copy in quantity and revise on a PC or by hand. The possibilities for tracking formats are infinite, so be careful to choose what best suits your needs and budget. Figure 6-3 on page 55 shows a tracking format for use on a PC.

As your prospect pool grows, you should consider purchasing a commercial database software package. Although the initial cost may seem burdensome, this investment will, in the long run, produce significant savings in staff time.

All systems, from the simple card file to the complex, integrated computerized system, are useful only if their data is updated through careful analysis and review on a regular and timely schedule. And all systems, particularly small, idiosyncratic systems, must be well documented, so that staff turnover doesn't result in a loss of valuable information.

Avoiding pitfalls: Coordination policies and practices

Several years ago, development staff at the University of Pennsylvania solicited a top prospect for a 25th reunion commitment, a gift to support the university's football program, and an endowed scholarship fund. All three solicitations occurred within a three-day period and were made by separate solicitors. Quite naturally, after this fund-raising "frontal assault," the prospect reported that he felt deluged. On the heels of this experience, the board chairperson and a dean visited another Penn prospect in rapid succession. Both solicitors requested that the prospect make a significant gift to the university.

Fortunately for Penn, both situations eventually resulted in successful solicitations, but only after considerable "damage control." Nevertheless, this example shows the harm that uncoordinated prospect management can wreak upon even the most well established development program.

Uncoordinated prospect efforts can confuse and frustrate major donor prospects to the extent that they may refuse to give to your institution or warn other donors away from offering support. Uncoordinated prospect management can also frustrate solicitation volunteers. Volunteers offer their time and energy for free. When "wire crossing" and miscommunication become the norm, and not the exception, to working for your institution, volunteers become disaffected and inactive.

These scenarios can be harmful to any institution's development effort, especially in the current climate of competing philanthropic interests and limited resources.

One coordination system: The Prospect Action Advisory Committee (PAAC)

After these near disasters, Penn's development office decided that its prospect management team needed to coordinate its activities much more closely. To do so, Penn created a new development tradition, the Prospect Action Advisory Committee (PAAC).

PAAC's goal is to coordinate all the parts of the prospect identification, cultivation, and solicitation process to ensure that prospects realize and offer their fullest gift potential. This kind of coordination ensures that staff and volunteers get "the best shot" at closing the maximum gift possible from a prospect. In this effort, PAAC does not impede individual development operations or undermine the entrepreneurial efforts of a given person or development area. Rather, PAAC enables the institution to put its best foot forward by using all the players on the development team effectively.

Coordination policies. PAAC's goals of coordination are to:
- promote purposeful cultivation that results in maximum support;
- enhance staff and volunteer relationships with prospects;
- reduce the incidence of confused and mixed messages among staff, volunteers, and prospects;
- strengthen the quality and consistency of staff-prospect contacts;
- facilitate the equitable distribution of prospects among staff and volunteers;
- encourage sustained and timely attention to the execution of planned cultivation/ solicitation strategies; and

• ensure that institutional fund-raising objectives take priority in major gift fund raising.

Coordination practices. Senior development officers experienced in prospect analysis and external relationships manage PAAC. These individuals represent all areas of the institution's development effort. For example, the director of capital giving serves as the PAAC chair. Development directors from the annual and planned giving, corporate and foundation relations, and academic and research departments serve as PAAC members. When necessary, support staff assist PAAC with gathering needed information. PAAC uses tracking data, individual records, relationship analyses, and other relevant materials to guide its coordination efforts.

During its bi-weekly meetings, PAAC uses its coordinating strength to:
• assign new prospects;
• consider prospect reassignment requests;
• re-evaluate prospect contacts;
• set the time line for the solicitation of prospects; and
• evaluate readiness and reassignment for second solicitations.

After making its recommendations to the senior vice president for development, these recommendations are distributed by memo to staff. Tracking staff enter PAAC assignments into the tracking system for execution and use by all development staff. See figure 6-4 on page 56 for an example of a PAAC information tracking form.

PAAC also handles those development "snafus" that can too often fall through the cracks and foul prospect management. For example, PAAC often "grandfathers in" prospects who already have a relationship with a specific area of the institution. When more than one academic area claims a relationship with a prospect, PAAC makes sure that this prospect is protected from conflicting requests.

The PAAC process is fluid. When necessary, members and staff may present a case for retaining a prospect beyond the time deadline. PAAC may make joint assignments for a single prospect, giving two or more areas the right to solicit a prospect with the understanding there will be communication before making contact. When conflicts occur, PAAC re-evaluates and changes assignments to meet the institution's needs and preserve the vitality of the prospect/institution relationship.

Benefits of establishing a PAAC at your institution. PAAC is a testimonial to the positive effect that organized coordination can have on your institution's major gift program. As Penn began planning its largest capital campaign, competition for access to prospects between the University's 12 schools and five resource centers threatened the campaign's success. To further ensnarl development efforts, the plethora of giving interests in Penn's support constituency signaled that potential donor ambivalence could diminish Penn's total return. Some alumni possessed degrees from different Penn schools; other donors expressed interest in supporting very different programs, such as the university's hospital and museum. PAAC stepped into this situation, coordinating various giving strategies and diffusing disasters before they exploded. Later, PAAC showed itself to be just as valuable as a day-to-day management tool.

Whether your development program is breaking down under the strain of uncoordinated efforts or not, it is a good idea to explore setting up a PAAC structure at your institution before problems occur. By using a coordinating structure like the PAAC, you can make optimal use of your program's computer resources and "people skills." Moreover, a coordinating structure inspires staff, volunteers, prospects, and donors to give their best efforts and generosity to your institution again and again.

Conclusion

Computer tracking and prospect coordination have changed the way development staff manage prospect outreach. Tracking systems help major gift officers acquire increased productivity and heightened performance. Tracking systems help staff understand large prospect pools whose members have broad and competing interests. By combining the appropriate tracking system for your institution with hands-on coordination, your development team can reach and positively affect today's broad and sought-after prospect pool.

As the not-so-old adage bears out: "Before there were cars, there wasn't a need for garages to service them." A mere decade ago, your development program might have successfully foregone the efficiency and effectiveness of a prospect tracking system and PAAC coordination. But in today's complex fund-raising environment, prospect tracking systems and coordination are here to stay. Like the mechanic's garage, they're no longer an option.

Figure 6-1: Central tracking data entry form

Contacts

Name: _____ I.D.: _____
Affiliation: _____
Area of Int: _____
Project Code: _____

Date: _____ Contact By: _____
Action: _____

_____

_____

Next Action: _____

_____

_____

By Staff: _____ By Date: _____

Contacts

Name: _____ I.D.: _____
Affiliation: _____
Area of Int: _____
Project Code: _____

Date: _____ Contact By: _____
Action: _____

_____

_____

Next Action: _____

_____

_____

By Staff: _____ By Date: _____

Figure 6-2: Prospect report—Summary to next steps

PROSPECT SUMMARY

Name:
I.D. #:   Source: A   Alumnus/a
Affiliation: CW-73, GR-76, Gxx-77
City, St (Country)   Philadelphia   Region Cde: PH
Related ID's:
Current Assignment: SAE
Capital Rating: $100,000
Areas of Interest: 1   SAS   English Department
                          2   ATH
                          3   ICA
                          4   SOS
                          5   SAS   English Department

Comments: Mother was a trustee in the 1940s. Has sizable real
                          estate holdings.

Other information:
Last update: 12/16/1988 By: rip count $S: 5 #C   9 #G: 1

    Next previous View Add Edit Del Status Contact Gift Bio
Display the next prospect for the current criteria selection.

PROSPECT STATUS

Name   ID:
Current Assignment: SAE
Area of Interest: SAS English Department   F 09/23/88
Project Code: 04001   English Dept. Faculty Devel-
                                                   opment
Gift Target: $100,000   Gift Type: cash
Primary Staff Reps: Randy   Secondary Staff: Carole
Gift Purpose: 03900   Faculty Travel/Research
                                                   Grants Solicitor:
Other Contacts:
Comments: Heavily committed to building good creative
                          writing program at Penn.
Last contact: 08/01/1988   By:
Last action: Followup letter after visit. Answered her question
                          about the number of students in poetry and fiction
                          classes at Penn.

Next contact: 8/22/1988   By:
Next action: Invitation to dinner (with her husband)

Next Previous View Add Edit Delete Contact Gift Help
Edit the current Prospect Status information.

PROSPECT CONTACT

Name   ID:
Affiliation: CW-73, GR-76, GSE-77
Area of Interest: SAS English Department   F 09/23/88
Project Code: 04001   English Dept. Faculty Development

Date: 08/01/1988
Contact By:

    Action: Follow up letter after visit. Answered her question about the
    number of students in poetry and fiction classes at Penn.

Next action: Invitation to Eisenhower dinner (with her husband)

    By Staff:
    By Date: 08/22/1988

  Next Previous View Add Edit delete Status-next-action-edit
Display the next Contact (in reverse chronological order.)

Figure 6-3: Tracking format for use on a personal computer (PC)

Name: ID#:   Type:

School(s) and Year(s):

City: State:

Authorized Access:

Gift Target: Capability Rating:

Gift Purpose: Gift Type:

Readiness: Gift Complete/Stewardship:

Interest Area(s):

School(s) or Center(s):

Solicitor: Staff responsibility:

Volunteers or Contacts:

Last Action Date:

Last Action:

Next Action Date:

Next Action:

Comments/Recent Gifts:

                                                        File Updated:

Figure 6-4: PAAC information tracking form

Requesting Area:

Prospect Name:

School(s) and Year(s):

ID#:

City and State:

Devsystem Giving Ability Rating:

Range of Proposed Gift:

Prosposed Area(s) of Support:

Summary and Nature of Past Relationship (Including Gift History):

Proposed Date and Nature of Next Action:

Comments:

Chapter 7

Prospect Identification and Assessment: Using Prospect Meetings and Peer Review

Linda J. Marks
Development Officer
Graduate School of Business
Stanford University
Stanford, California

Development officers know that roughly 90 to 95 percent of the total funds given to an institution come from 5 to 10 percent of our donors. This small group of people can really make the difference between a healthy flow of support and an embattled development effort. Therefore, we give top priority to finding and cultivating the major donor constituency. Prospect identification and assessment are key steps to discovering major donors for future contact. These steps will tell you:

- the identities of your best prospects;
- the locations of your best prospects;
- the level of giving that you can expect from these prospects;
- the projects and programs that they are most likely to support;
- the most appropriate solicitor; and
- the allocation of staff and financial resources that will result in productive marketing and fund-raising activities.

Most institutions use several methods to identify and assess prospects. In-house assessment utilizes the knowledge, skills, and resources of fund raisers and research staff to target prospects. Electronic screening uses geographic and demographic data to produce computer analyses of prospective donors. Another method uses volunteers to provide anecdotal but valuable information on prospects that major donor officers can use in future solicitation efforts. This "horse's mouth" approach of prospect identification can take several forms, including screening sessions and peer reviews.

Screening sessions are prospect meetings where development staff and volunteers bring together friends of the institution to review lists of possible future donors. These friends can be alumni, past major donors, or other interested philanthropists. Most important is that these friends can review donor lists and offer their informed assessment as to the viability of targeting specific new donors. Peer review uses the same screening method, but limits the assessors and the assessed to a limited pool of individuals. For example, a group of alumni might conduct a peer review of other alumni.

Stanford University has used screening sessions and peer reviews to significantly increase major donor participation. One of our more aggressive screening efforts occurred in the mid 1980s. During a period of 18 months, we conducted 133 screening sessions in cities across the country where many of our alumni and friends lived. This ambitious effort involved 2,400 volunteer screeners.

Not every institution can afford such an approach. The approach you choose should fit your institution's development objectives and available resources.

Setting objectives

Before initiating a prospect review and assessment program, you must decide what you hope to accomplish. What are your objectives? You may wish to re-evaluate your existing population of rated prospects. Identifying additional, new prospects may also be a critical goal. You may want to use the impetus of a capital campaign or upcoming class reunions to validate your reasons for prospecting. Perhaps your prospect identification program will focus on graduates of single departments or particular classes, or on graduates living in a certain community.

Our objective was to screen the alumni and appropriate nonalumni population, with particular attention to those who had graduated in the previous 20 years. Alumni included graduates of all schools and departments. Our sessions involved a mix of alumni and other friends who volunteered to screen our lists. We did not undertake to identify corporate or foundation donors, nor did we attempt to assess inclination through our screening sessions.

In addition to identifying large gift donors, a prospect identification and assessment program can identify potential volunteers who may be able to offer their expertise and help to your major gift program. Whatever your objectives, once started, a prospect identification and assessment program must be ongoing. Your staff and volunteers should remain alert for those individuals with greater gift potential.

Assessing resources

Several resources will shape the organization and success of a prospect identification and assessment program.

Staff. Is the size of your staff adequate to manage your program and conduct prospect identification sessions? To support Stanford's program, we hired a full-time director of prospecting, an assistant director, and a secretary for the term of the project. In addition, we added screening session tasks to the duties of 60 other development staff members.

Volunteers. Will staff conduct your prospect review, or will you call upon volunteers to assist the screening process? An established group of committed volunteers can get your screening sessions off to a good start

What roles and responsibilities will your volunteers assume? There were two volunteer roles in our program, the host and the screener. You should consider carefully:

- how you will enlist volunteers;
- whom you will enlist for each role; and
- how you will involve existing and new volunteers.

How many volunteers do you need to invite or enlist in order to have a sufficient number of individuals at each session? We found that, in order to have 20 to 25 attendees at each session, we needed to invite at least four times that number.

Computer support. Is your computer system adequate to produce lists, track names, and correlate results? Can staff use the system themselves or does it require special expertise? Your computer system will be integral and essential to the success of your prospecting program. Without database and technical staff support, we could not have undertaken a timely, personalized program. To ensure this support, we allocated two-thirds of the program's nonsalary budget for computer services.

Time. Allow adequate time to plan and execute your prospecting effort. The Stanford program required a year of planning and 18 months for execution. The amount of time you need will vary depending on the number of names you must review, the number of sessions needed, and the number of available staff.

In addition, the urgency for information will dictate timing. In one instance, you may need to complete your prospecting project before starting a campaign. In another instance, your program deadline may be more flexible.

Budget. Several costs will vary with the scope of your project. If you choose to run peer review sessions, think creatively about ways to share costs with other areas of your institution. For example, you may be able to share the costs of travel and meals. To lower speakers' costs, you can enlist faculty and staff members who were already traveling to the screening session site for other purposes. To help defray some expenses, you might consider asking your volunteers to donate some or all of the costs of a session.

A prescription for effective screening and peer review sessions

Several elements will help your sessions run smoothly, while maximizing the amount of useful information they produce:

Logistics. Where will you hold your screening sessions? Sessions can occur on campus, in private homes, or at other reception sites. You should be sensitive to locations that may discriminate on the basis of race, sex, or religion.

When do you schedule the session? At Stanford, we found that volunteers preferred to attend early evening sessions held between 4:30 and 7:30 p.m.

How long will your sessions last? We scheduled two-hour meetings with one hour allotted for reviewing the prospect list of 2,000 names.

Will the screening sessions include a meal? Will specific sessions feature a speaker or other presentation? These elements will rely on the availability of staff and program funds.

Who will handle the arrangements for your sessions? We divided the responsibilities for each of Stanford's screening sessions among the program staff, session staff, and host. The chart illustrated in Figure 7-1 on page 61 shows how we delineated screening session responsibilities:

Ratings. How many times should volunteers review each name? Our goal was to have each name reviewed five times. In practice, volunteers reviewed the names of graduates from the 1960s and later an average of 10 times.

How many validations do you need to feel comfortable about a prospect's capacity to give? You may want to convert multiple estimates of giving capacity into a single rating. For this purpose, you may need to develop a range of ratings or rating codes. You will also need to decide whether volunteers will provide ratings silently or share their judgments openly.

Screening Lists. What criteria will you use to select names for screening? You can use class year, academic major, geographic location, and other criteria to target list names.

What format should your lists take? You should make sure that the information displayed in the list will help your volunteers in making their assessments. However, you should not provide information that may influence the ratings. Excess information, such as an address on a wealthy street, might lead a screener to make incorrect assumptions about an individual's capacity to give.

How many names can volunteers screen in the time you have allowed? We found that our screeners could review and rate a list of 2,000 names in an hour. The information provided was limited to name, degree, year of graduation, and city and state of residence.

Is there other information you want your screeners to provide? You may want to ask screening volunteers to rate the inclination and philanthropic interests of prospects, as well as estimate each prospect's capacity to give.

Materials. What kinds of reports will help you organize and assimilate the rating information once you have gathered it? We developed three report formats to convey our assessments:

1. a *prospect report* showed the ratings received by a prospect and identified the screeners who made them;

2. a *screener report* listed the prospects who each screener reviewed and the ratings they gave; and

3. a *rating report* charted the prospects by their ratings and listed their screeners.

Remember, there is no right answer in rating or judging a prospect's capacity to make a major gift. Only after you combine your best guess, the opinions of your volunteers, and appropriate public information will you be able to arrive at a reliable estimate of a prospect's capacity to give.

Prospect identification and assessment can be a very ambitious undertaking. Thoughtful planning and careful execution of screening and peer review programs will produce results that can significantly benefit your institution.

Figure 7-1: Screening session timetable

ACTIVITY	PROGRAM STAFF RESPONSIBILITIES	SESSION STAFF RESPONSIBILITIES	HOST RESPONSIBILITIES	PROPOSED COMPLETION DATE
Perform internal research for prospective host.	Provide computer support to develop names of potential hosts.	Provide personal knowledge to develop names of potential hosts.		5-6 months prior to screening session.
Perform internal research for prospective screeners.	Provide computer support to develop names of potential participants.	Provide personal knowledge to develop names of potential participants.		4-6 months prior to screening session.
Recruit host to coordinate local screening session.	Send thank-you/ confirmation letter from individual who made the enlistment.	Send own thank-you letter with program description and list of potential screeners.		3 months prior to screening session.
Schedule proposed date for screening session.	Develop master schedule with guidelines for timing of screening sessions.	Work with host to identify location and set date/time for screening session, within time frame of master schedule.	Work with session staff to identify location and set time/date for screening session. Provide session staff with names of local friends to be invited.	

ACTIVITY	PROGRAM STAFF RESPONSIBILITIES	SESSION STAFF RESPONSIBILITIES	HOST RESPONSIBILITIES	PROPOSED COMPLETION DATE
Finalize time and place for screening session.		Session staff to confirm with host.		2-3 months prior to screening session.
Invite participants to screening session.	Prepare and send invitations. Track invitations: a) yes, will attend; b) unable to attend; and c) no response.	Work with program staff to track invitations. Keep host informed about responses.	Work with session to identify key people for more personal (phone) invitation. Phone key people to encourage their participation.	5-6 months prior to screening session. Before or concurrently with the invitation mailing.
Follow up on invitations.	a) Yes: send confirmation from host. b) Unable to attend: send courtesy thank-you letter from host. Invite to a later session. c) No response: coordinate follow up by phone.	Determine the host's best way to follow up on non-respondents.	Work with session staff to coordinate follow up to non-respondents.	As soon as feasible, once status is known.

ACTIVITY	PROGRAM STAFF RESPONSIBILITIES	SESSION STAFF RESPONSIBILITIES	HOST COMPLETION	PROPOSED COMPLETION DATE
Finalize arrangements for screening session.	Request screening lists from computer.			3 weeks prior to screening session.
	Finalize screening session materials and mail to host.			2 weeks prior to screening session.
		Work with host to finalize arrangements at location. Materials arrive.	Work with session staff on final arrangements for screening session.	1 week prior to screening session.
Hold screening session.		Staff screening session.	Chair screening session.	
Screening session clean up.	Prepare "at home" packets for participants who: a) did not screen total class lists; or b) requested other geographical or class lists.	Send thank-you letter to host. Return session materials to program staff.	Make personal (phone) thank-you to some screeners. Send pre-printed thank you cards to all screeners.	Immediately after screening session.
	Input rating info into computer tracking system.			Upon receipt of lists.
	Send final report to all participants on results of screening.			12-18 months after screening session.

Chapter 8

Using Volunteers in the Major Gift Program

David G. Pond
Assistant Headmaster, Alumni Affairs and Development
Deerfield Academy
Deerfield, Massachusetts

A nyone who has run a nonprofit organization can tell you just how valuable volunteers can be. Whether they stuff envelopes, write articles for your newsletter, serve as board members, or play the role of peacemaker between your institution and a disillusioned funder, volunteers can be the backbone of any organization. When misdirected or undertrained, however, volunteers can also break the back of any of your best-laid development plans. Therefore, it is very important to develop a clear plan for working with volunteers and directing their efforts. A straightforward plan, which is mutually understood by staff and volunteers, will keep your major gift volunteers "on track," diffuse needless conflict, and strengthen your volunteers' loyalty to your institution.

Most people who work as volunteers do so because they would like to forward a cause, combat a social ill, or nurture the growth of a cherished institution. Volunteers are driven by their desire *to make a difference*. A successful major gift volunteer program gives individuals the opportunity to do just that. Because major gifts make up an overwhelming share of the dollars raised by an institution, involvement in the major gift process gives volunteers a critical role in the advancement of your institution.

Developing a plan for major gift volunteers

Organizing and directing major gift volunteers should be an ongoing priority of any major gift program. However, certain development activities lend themselves to strengthening a volunteer network. In particular, campaigns are logical and advantageous times for establishing and enlarging major gift volunteer programs. The preparation of a campaign brings staff and volunteers together, focuses their activities on a very specific and important effort, and gives everyone delegated roles and responsibilities in a team effort.

Creating a campaign time line is a particularly good place to formulate your volunteer plan. The time line should include pre-campaign events, kickoff events, various campaign gatherings, and a concluding event. More important, the time line should detail your plan for involving major gift volunteers in these and other campaign activities. During the time line preparation process, you can begin to define volunteer involvement.

To accurately and comprehensively plan volunteer involvement, you should address a few key questions. I have outlined several of these questions here, however you may also want to add your own priority questions to this list. This Q & A exercise will not only help you formulate your plan, but may also help you to anticipate questions that will be posed to you later by major gift volunteers.

What are the qualities of effective, engaged major gift volunteers?

The qualities most prized in major gift volunteers are involvement, influence, income, and interest.

Involvement. Meaningful involvement is perhaps the most important qualification for a major gift volunteer. The best volunteers are those individuals who have already involved themselves with your institution or who have dedicated their skills previously to nonprofit service. Such a "track record" demonstrates that the volunteer possesses a high capacity for commitment. Moreover, it may indicate that the volunteer is active in the fund-raising community, in general, and in the major gift constituency, specifically.

Look for major gift volunteers on the advisory boards and other advancement fora of your institution. Such places include departmental advisory boards, governing boards of alumni groups, gift clubs, and recognition societies. Past service as fund-raising volunteers is an excellent indicator of a major gift volunteer in the making.

Influence. Major gift volunteers should also be influential members of the group they will lead. Even though volunteers do not usually serve as the lead solicitor, they do play a critical role in many solicitations. Stature within the major gift community, combined with the commitment they evidence by making their own gifts, will increase your volunteers' effectiveness as fund raisers for your institution.

Income. Income is a shorthand way of saying that major gift volunteers should have the financial capacity and personal willingness to make a major gift themselves. Ideally, a major gift volunteer should have already made significant commitment to your organization in the past. Although this gift may not have been the largest one made for a particular priority, it should be at or above the level of a sacrifice that they will be asking of others.

Interest. Major gift volunteers should possess a keen interest in fund raising. Volunteers should consider their role in making and facilitating solicitations both refreshing and challenging. When they possess this fund-raising viewpoint, volunteers are better able to weather the inevitable highs and lows of the campaign and in their own fund-raising work.

Having volunteers who are interested in fund raising is important; keeping these special volunteers interested in offering their development prowess is critical. Therefore, you must make rejuvenating and maintaining volunteer interest a top priority of your volunteer plan. You can do this by targeting individual interests and preferences, and assigning duties accordingly. Some volunteers may enjoy building an endowment; others prefer bricks and mortar projects. Give assignments to volunteers in areas that appeal to them personally. This will inspire your volunteers, increase their confidence in their own ability "to do the work," and increase the overall success of your volunteer network. With a little preliminary investigation, you will probably be able to fit the interests of your volunteers with your funding needs list.

What is the best way to find major gift volunteers?

Individuals who have served in previous volunteer capacities or who currently hold leadership roles are the people who are most likely to serve again. However, it's a mistake to limit your search for volunteers to the individuals already in the volunteer pool. In other words, do not rely solely on those who "have already done their duty." Cultivating new volunteers and helping current volunteers improve their skills will help to maintain the health of your volunteer effort for years to come.

Campaigns offer a real opportunity to test the metal of your volunteer management abilities. It is usually a good rule of thumb to look for new leadership for each new campaign. Deerfield recently completed a campaign that exceeded its dollar goal by 16 percent. The leader was 32 years old when he kicked off this successful campaign. In the world of effective volunteer fund raisers, age certainly does not come before ability.

In order to find new, energetic volunteers, investigate your institution's support organizations. Look for volunteers in your institution's alumni, class agent, and parent organizations. Donors to recent campaigns (who were not campaign volunteers) may also be interested in offering their volunteer skills. When searching for new volunteers, keep your eyes open for individuals of stature who will attract both good volunteers and critical major gift support.

The best intentions may not always produce timely results. Some volunteers may be sufficiently committed, but may lack the grace, ability, or sheer "stick-to-it-ness" to get the job done. When you are creating a major gift committee, look for the good workers first. Experience shows that individuals who have the time, discipline, and real desire to see a task to completion will find a way to get it done.

How should my institution recruit major gift volunteers?

Once you identify your list of possible candidates, you will need to get to know these individuals better. This is especially true when you recruit prospective volunteers with whom you have not worked previously. At this stage, your aim is to create a relationship among your staff, the volunteers, and you that makes everyone feel comfortable and empowered.

Asking a volunteer to serve. How you ask a volunteer to serve will also set the tone of your volunteer program. A key trustee, campaign leader, or the head of the institution should offer the request to serve in person. Never make these requests casually or without the utmost demeanor of respect. Everything about the request should demonstrate the importance of the task at hand, as well as the institution's appreciation of the volunteer's commitment. Follow up each request with a written description of the volunteer's job and responsibilities. The description may also state the number of solicitations that the volunteer should expect to complete.

Explaining volunteer workloads. At the outset, let volunteers know how much time they will be expected to commit to their work. Time is a precious commodity for most major gift volunteers. Therefore, do not underestimate the amount of time needed to complete even a short list of solicitations. In addition to personal visits, solicitations may require extensive phone calls, follow-up letters, and the organization of campaign events. All these activities have the potential to be extremely time-consuming. Therefore, be realistic in describing to major gift volunteers the time they will need to commit to their work. Whenever possible, familiarize volunteers with staff support that will be available to them.

Once all the major gift volunteers are "on board," you are ready to begin their education to become solicitors for your institution.

How will we get major gift volunteers involved in the process?

The sooner that you can involve major gift volunteers in the campaign planning process, the better. A regular flow of information to all volunteers should begin as soon as possible and continue throughout the campaign. Keep volunteers apprised of the campaign's progress. Share with them the list of your major gift prospects. A screening meeting to review your major prospect list will give each major gift volunteer a sense of the scope of the campaign and the prospects it hopes to reach.

Seek the counsel and advice of volunteers before you finalize your needs list. Although you may know the needs of your institution thoroughly, volunteers may know the fund-raising landscape better than you do. Volunteers can be helpful in identifying which of your needs are likely to receive the warmest reception from major gift donors.

Training volunteers. Because volunteers serve as ambassadors of your institution, you will want them to be well informed. Volunteers should understand your campaign's needs, and should see those needs firsthand. Therefore, as soon as possible, bring your major gift volunteers to campus for an orientation and training session. Your institution does not need to underwrite the volunteers' travel expenses, but it should cover all of their on-campus expenses.

Volunteers who know your institution and the campaign thoroughly will be best-equipped to answer questions and concerns raised by prospects during solicitations. The questions that volunteers most commonly ask concern the school's budget, endowment, admissions policy, job placement, and changes in the curriculum. You should convey this information in a clear and concise manner, in order that volunteers can handle questions regarding these topics thoroughly and appropriately.

Address any controversial topics, whether potential or actual, at the onset, especially if you want to ensure that these topics are handled delicately, but uniformly. You may want to provide a brief position paper on a troublesome subject, which the volunteers can leave with prospects for their private review. The purpose of this paper, as well as the training and orientation process, is to make your volunteers feel confident and comfortable about the solicitation process.

Keep the solicitation training short and fun. Role-playing in practice solicitations, which can be educational and entertaining, is an effective way to give your volunteers practical experience in asking for gifts. Volunteers should also get some experience in *being* asked for gifts. At some point during the session, inform your volunteers that you will be asking each of them for his or her support as soon as possible after the session. Therefore, any questions that *they* have should be addressed now.

During the early training sessions, you may find that some volunteers may not be well suited for a particular volunteer role. The sooner you act on this knowledge, the better. To remedy "mismatches," meet with the volunteer to discuss your concerns that his or her skills are not being used to their full potential. Be prepared to take extra care in making assignments for that volunteer. In all dealings with volunteers, it will be necessary to be at your diplomatic best!

What are reasonable workloads for major gift volunteers?

Keep major gift assignment lists short. Some major gift volunteers may only do one solicitation; most volunteers will complete three or four. Nevertheless, allow each volunteer to assume no more than two solicitations at a time. Solicitations must be personal and of a high quality. Therefore, it is better to err on the side of quality, rather than volume, when assigning solicitations to volunteers.

Be sure that you review each solicitation with the major gift volunteer beforehand. Is the volunteer reasonably comfortable with executing this solicitation? Does the volunteer have all of the prospect information that you can provide? You should allow for a reasonable period of time for the completion of each solicitation. Two to four weeks is a reasonable "start to finish" period for solicitations. Each solicitation may require more than one visit. Therefore, encourage volunteers to arrange appointments with prospects as quickly as possible.

Although most solicitations work best one on one, there may be times when you, as the fund-raising professional, should be included in the process. Generally, that decision should be left to the volunteer.

What other tasks should volunteers undertake?

Presenting written proposals. Providing written proposals to prospects before, during, and after the solicitation, can help the solicitation's progress significantly. Busy prospects may find it easier to respond to a solicitation in a reasonable amount of time if they have something in writing to consider. Written proposals also increase the effectiveness of follow-up calls by giving the caller and the prospect common ground to discuss. Provide your volunteers with written proposals and train them to present them in a timely and appropriate manner.

Following up on completed solicitations. Once a pledge or gift has been made, there are two final tasks for the volunteer: the thank-you letter and the final solicitation report. The volunteer should draft and send a thank-you letter to the donor he or she has solicited successfully, and send a copy of the letter to you for development tracking. Equally critical to the solicitation process is the final solicitation report. The volunteer should prepare and submit his or her final report to you as soon as possible after the completed solicitation, in order that important facts do not become stale or forgotten. This report may be oral or written. Because your institution will likely solicit the donor in the future, the information gleaned from the final solicitation report will undoubtedly be helpful to your development team.

How should my institution reward volunteers for their efforts?

Campaigns offer several avenues for recognizing and thanking the hard-working major gift volunteer. You may recognize volunteers for their diligent efforts in campaign publications or at public campaign events. Personalized letters of thanks and commendations, which are suitable for framing, from your institution's president or the chair of the board of trustees are tangible reminders of a volunteer's excellent service. In addition, you may want to establish a two-tiered program for recognizing volunteer service. Under such a recognition program, deserving volunteers receive one award for service within a given year and another award for lifetime achievement. Establish and maintain high standards for both awards so that they convey prestige and respect for the volunteers receiving them.

What are the benefits of cultivating and involving major gift volunteers?

Enlisting volunteers in your major gift effort can offer a number of benefits to your campaign and development efforts. A network of capable volunteers will increase the number of solicitations that you can complete. In addition, the use of peer-to-peer gift requests is an effective form of fund raising. Beyond their ability to perform individual asks, however, volunteers can add credibility to all your development efforts. A cadre of volunteers willing to invest their own time, energy, and resources in your institution is a powerful and persuasive statement on the worthiness of your fund-raising goals.

There are other reasons why enlisting major gift volunteers is so beneficial. First, serving in the volunteer program provides an opportunity to educate individuals, not only as volunteers, but also as major gift prospects and donors, in a meaningful way. The greater their prior involvement with your institution, the greater the likelihood donors will provide maximum support to your institution when they are asked for a gift. A background of volunteer fund raising for your institution is an excellent way to expose a prospective donor to your institution and to the idea of giving a major gift in the future.

Second, major gift volunteers are people of stature who will attract other donors to your institution. Each of your institution's major gift volunteers defines the very best of what your institution represents. Influential major donor volunteers cultivate your institution's position within the funding community and among other major donors.

Third, volunteer experience in major gift work builds and strengthens relationships between your institution and donors. Today's volunteers will be some of your best prospects for future campaigns. In fact, much of the support for any campaign comes from previous major gift volunteers.

Conclusion

As you prepare to recruit your next group of major gift volunteers, keep in mind these key points, and you will gain an invaluable resource to help ensure the success of your campaign and the future prosperity of your institution:

1. Volunteers prefer meaningful, challenging tasks that are part of a clear, concise plan.

2. Look for "fresh" volunteer leaders who have provided high-quality volunteer service to your institution or other organizations in the past.

3. Regularly involve major gift volunteers in campaign planning.

4. Expect that each volunteer will be able to make a major gift to your campaign.

5. Keep lists of assignments and completion times short.

6. Thank your major gift volunteers in a thoughtful and meaningful way.

Chapter 9

Narrowing the Major Gift Market: Principal Gifts

William F. Dailey
Principal Gift Director, Emeritus
Stanford University
Stanford, California

Lucretia L. Martin
Special Assistant to the President
Dartmouth University
Hanover, New Hampshire

Dennis J. Caplis
Writer
Fremont, Michigan

A $5-million gift, a $15-million gift, a $30-million gift, gifts large enough to propel a campaign, create a program, or endow a school—these are gifts that development dreams are made of. To make those dreams come true, many institutions have established principal gift programs. Through these efforts, institutions give their highest-rated prospects the time and attention they expect, deserve, and require before and after making multi-million dollar commitments. At Stanford and Dartmouth we have found that a principal gift program can offer a gratifying return on fund-raising dollars invested.

Every school should have systems in place to maximize its top prospects' involvement with and support for the institution. To help you determine if your institution could also benefit from a dedicated principal gift effort, we have posed and answered some fundamental questions about this development approach.

The ideas discussed here may be of interest to you even if your prospect pool is small and the resources available to expand your development program are smaller still.

What is the definition of a principal gift?

The dollar range of principal gifts depends on the gift range covered by the program immediately below the proposed principal gift program. If your major gift program seeks gifts in the $100,000- to $1-million range, your principal gift program could target gifts in the $3- to $5-million range. Large universities generally define principal gifts as $5-million and above. Alternatively, you could define principal gift prospects as the top 2 percent of your potential donors.

In setting the principal gift level, however, it is important to create a prospect pool that the principal gift officer can reasonably manage. Securing multi-million dollar gifts is time-intensive work, both before and after the gifts are made. Therefore, no principal gift officer should be expected to work with more than 50 prospects.

Does your organization need a principal gift program?

First, decide your principal gift level and determine how many prospects you have in that gift range. If your institution is not realizing the gift potential of these individuals, you should consider establishing a principal gift program. When analyzing available prospects, do not overlook nonalumni in your area, especially wealthy persons with no other college allegiance.

What factors are vital to a successful principal gift program?

To institute a successful principal gift program, your institution should meet certain basic conditions:

• The president of your institution must participate fully in the program and offer his or her leadership. If he or she is unwilling or unable to cultivate and solicit principal gift prospects, you should not begin a program.

• Your institution must also make at least a five-year financial commitment to the principal gift effort.

• The program must have the support of your major gift staff and the respect of other constituencies in your institution.

How does principal gift fund raising differ from major gift work?

Though the fundamental fund-raising steps remain much the same, having fewer prospects allows the principal gift officer to do more in-depth strategic planning and to spend much more time personalizing the contacts with prospects. Though major gift work uses a personalized approach, its sheer volume of prospects necessarily makes major gift fund raising less time-intensive and more volunteer-oriented.

What is the profile of a principal gift prospect?

In general, principal gift prospects have provided for their families' future financial needs and have a strong interest in education, a special interest in a particular field, and an extensive record of giving. They often, but not always, have a desire for recognition.

More specifically, from 1983 to 1988 the principal gift donors at Stanford were generally 65 to 75 years of age, married only once, and were the founders (or the descendants of the founders) of very successful businesses. All had served as trustees of major educational institutions and had long records of previous gifts.

How much wealth should an individual have to be considered a principal gift prospect?

The rule of thumb for a principal gift prospect is that their disposable net worth should be 10 to 20 times larger than your principal gift level. For example, if your principal gift level is $5 million, a prospect should possess a net worth of $50 to $100 million. Generally, people who possess a high current income level with relatively few capital assets are not good candidates for principal gifts.

In some cases, the threshold net worth of a principal gift prospect could be much lower. Special circumstances may come into play that enable the prospect to give a principal gift. For example, a prospect may be able to give a principal gift if he or she is very old and has no family.

What steps should your organization take to implement a principal gift program?

Obviously, an organization must take the steps necessary to cultivate donors, solicit their support, and provide stewardship for their gifts and the donor/institution relationship. The president must commit his or her support to the program, which must include being available to the principal gift officer. Senior administrators must articulate the goals for the program and commit the resources needed to reach those goals. The development leadership must involve the major gift staff in devising a plan for prospect allocation and appoint a principal gift officer. This individual must be respected throughout the university and development community, and possess a successful fund-raising record.

What is the role of the principal gift officer?

The principal gift officer identifies those individuals in the prospect pool who are most able and most likely to give principal gifts, and facilitates the process of moving those prospects toward solicitations. Tasks of the principal gift officer may include:
- gathering information about prospects from their peers;
- selecting the most appropriate volunteers to pave the way for the president's contact with prospects;
- preparing personalized visits to campus for prospects; and
- coordinating special materials and presentations.

Moreover, the principal gift officer may have the primary responsibility for the stewardship of gifts after they have been made.

Under ideal circumstances, the principal gift officer should have no subordinates to manage and no duties other than fund raising. He or she should report to the vice president for development and have direct access to the president. In the real world, the principal gift officer may have to "wear more than one hat." However, a principal gift program will be most productive when its officer is free to concentrate fully on principal gift activities.

Does the principal gift officer meet and work with prospects directly?

Sometimes principal gift officers work directly with prospects. Generally, the primary role of the principal gift officer is to manage the process so that others have the most frequent and important contact with the prospects. More frequent contact between the prospect and the officer may occur if the principal gift officer has the duty of reporting on the use of the gift.

What is the role of the president with principal gift prospects?

In virtually all cases, the president should make the ask. If the solicitation is successful, he or she should remain the primary campus contact for the donor. Again, the participation of the president is essential to the success of a principal gift program.

What is the role of volunteers in principal gift fund raising?

External volunteers rarely ask for a principal gift. Their primary role is to add their personal knowledge of the prospect to planning strategy. If volunteers are particularly close to the prospect, they may help in opening the door for the university officer who will make the ultimate ask. Occasionally, volunteers may "test the waters" with a prospect, but they should not make the solicitation. A true principal gift prospect expects the leader of the institution to make the ask.

What are some effective ways of cultivating principal gift prospects?

There are several ways to cultivate principal gift prospects and encourage their involvement with your institution. One effective way is to ask prospects to serve as "consultants" for the long-range planning of the institution and for major projects they may support.

At Dartmouth we organized a very successful prospect planning group, called the President's Advisory Committee on Long-Range Planning. Donors serve two-year terms on the committee, but are often involved in its activities long after their terms expire. In fact, members of the early committees now hold reunions to monitor the institution's progress. It is not unusual for the husbands and wives of donors to serve on the committee with their spouses.

What is the best way to open communication with prospects who are guarded or wary?

Some prospects may have many philanthropic pursuits; others may be pursued by an overwhelming number of charitable causes. For whatever reason, donors may be guarded, ambivalent, or generally uncomfortable about opening a relationship with your institution.

The best way to "open the door" with such donors is to enlist the help of a trusted peer to intervene on your institution's behalf. The peer might be a trustee of your institution who knows the prospect or an adviser to the prospect who is an alumnus of your school. For added credibility with the prospect, your volunteer should have a generous giving record of his or her own.

If the volunteer is successful in "opening the door" between the prospect and your institution, the principal gift officer should make it a top priority to protect the privacy of the prospect.

Does principal gift work require special material such as publications or special naming opportunities?

Special publications for a given prospect are relatively rare. Special one-time proposals with expensive back-up material, such as scale models or custom drawings, are more common. Because of the magnitude of most principal gifts, your institution should tailor naming opportunities to meet the needs of the donor and the institution. The key word in principal gifts is "personalized."

If a principal gift prospect has little to no giving record with the institution, what is the best solicitation strategy to take?

If a principal gift prospect has no prior gift record, the odds are low that you will attract a principal gift from that person. Almost all principal gifts are made by persons who have been steadily increasing their gifts to an institution and are now at the peak of their wealth accumulation. If you do decide to ask a nondonor for a principal gift, you should not ask for a small gift. Rather, your request should be for a high-level gift. You may also want to enlist the help of a peer of the institution who has already made a gift at the same level. This peer may help encourage the new donor to make a similar commitment.

Are principal gifts generally paid out in cash or securities, over several years, or through trusts and bequests?

Many principal gifts are paid with appreciated assets transferred over a three-to-five-year period. Often these assets are negotiable securities. The funding of other principal gifts can be much more complex. They may entail a combination of payment methods such as securities from the individual, cash from a foundation controlled by the donor, or funds from a charitable trust. In general, larger gifts require a greater number of instruments to fund the commitment.

Conclusion

With the strong support of your institution's leadership, a principal gift program can be an effective and efficient way of realizing the full potential of your highest-rated prospects. It offers those prospects meaningful involvement in the life of your institution, while directing their generosity to where it is needed most. Just one or two principal gift successes can invigorate your development program and your institution. Always time-intensive, and often glacially slow, the principal gift process still offers rewards that are well worth the effort.

Chapter 10

An Effective Model of A Principal Gift Program

William H. Boardman Jr.
Director, University Capital Giving
Harvard University
Cambridge, Massachusetts

Principal gifts represent years, and in many cases, decades of relationship building between individuals and an institution. By the time an individual seriously considers making a leadership gift, the senior development officer's role is one of facilitator. He or she acts as a liaison, enabling individuals to accomplish what in their minds they have set out to do: influence an important cause they care deeply about through a truly significant investment.

An increasing number of institutions have recently established or strengthened principal gift programs that involve alumni and friends with the highest gift potential. Institutions now clearly recognize that securing multi-million dollar gifts from even their most devoted supporters demands significantly more time and effort than was previously allotted.

The senior development officers responsible for building relationships with major gift prospects are too frequently burdened with competing management, budgetary concerns, and other responsibilities, such as resolving admissions issues or organizing alumni events. The result: senior fund raisers are distracted from the critical task of working with their institution's highest-rated prospects.

Harvard learned this lesson during The Harvard Campaign (1979–1985). In this $350 million drive, the largest gift received was a $9 million gift—a relatively disappointing maximum gift amount considering the potential gift capacity of the Harvard's alumni and friends. Although the campaign was a success, Harvard did not break through to an appropriate gift level. To reach this new level, Harvard established the Office of University Capital Giving with responsibility for securing principal gifts (defined at Harvard as those of $5 million or more).

Essential ingredients for a successful principal gift program

During the 10 years since Harvard established its principal gift program, four ingredients have been vital to its success: a campaign atmosphere, identified gift opportunities, donor involvement, and a strong commitment of the president to principal gift fund raising These elements must be present and supported by any institution's leadership wanting to create an effective principal gift program.

A campaign atmosphere. Campaigns provide a potent reason—even an excuse, if you will—to communicate with alumni and friends with the greatest gift potential. An active campaign enables you to: ask prospects for their advice regarding planning issues; educate prospects about the greatest needs of the institution; and create an opportunity for prospects to make a large gift.

Identified gift opportunities. On a fairly regular basis, every institution should conduct a rigorous academic or program-planning process that results in a list of compelling priorities. In short, there must be a clear set of institutional goals and concrete plans for their fulfillment. Most donors give major gifts for a particular purpose; very few donors make large, unrestricted gifts.

Donor involvement. For the most part, people making principal gifts have histories of involvement with the institutions to which they give. Involvement, in this context, means "surviving" on the board of trustees or some similar governing board, working as a volunteer, or having longstanding relationships with the president or other leaders of the institution. Rarely will people make serendipitous gifts—large commitments made after an institutional relationship of only a few months. Alumni and friends who are involved in the life of the institution will not only know its priorities, but may also play a role in determining them. People that are engaged and involved also tend to raise their sights independently to increasingly higher gift levels.

Involving alumni and friends can take imagination. Harvard, for example, does not have the customary board of trustees. In order to involve its leading alumni and friends in institutional governance, Harvard established a number of academic planning committees, dean's councils, and advisory committees in areas such as student aid and international programs.

One extremely successful involvement vehicle has been Harvard's Committee on University Resources. This 400-member committee addresses university-wide fund-raising matters. The members are influential, generous, and prestigious alumni and friends who serve as an invaluable reservoir of volunteers and financial support. From this blue-ribbon group, Harvard elects a 34-member executive board. High on the list of selection criteria for election to this prestigious board is the capacity to make, and the capability to secure, principal gifts.

The executive board meets four times a year with the president, provost, and selected deans and also holds an annual two-day retreat. These gatherings give the president frequent opportunities to establish personal relationships with Harvard's potentially most important alumni and friends (from a development perspective) by seeking their counsel on fund-raising and academic planning issues.

A strong commitment from the president. This is the most important of the four ingredients. If the president does not devote ample time to advancing the principal gift process, then the program is destined to fail. The president must set aside time to meet with development staff to develop principal gift strategies, and to get to know key alumni and friends capable of making major gifts. The president's relationship with these individuals must extend well beyond the fund-raising context—and that demands time.

For virtually all influential alumni and friends, having a strong relationship with the president is a prerequisite to making a lifetime or ultimate gift. Building such a relationship with donors requires a commitment of time and energy from the president. In his first year in office, Harvard University President Neil Rudenstine met individually with more than 100 principal gift prospects. In addition, the president met with alumni and other individuals serving on committees, and attended events both on and off campus. The president frequently holds small dinners at his home for donors and special friends. Many of these evenings and events have a social, rather than a fund-raising, overtone.

Achieving this quantity and quality of interaction with key alumni and friends creates relationships that enable the president and individual donors to feel comfortable discussing large gifts. Frequently, such gifts evolve naturally out of this relationship.

With this foundation, a development officer, knowledgeable about the institution and its alumni and friends, can offer the greatest possible return on each dollar invested in the principal gift program.

Managing a principal gift program

At Harvard, the director of principal gifts simultaneously manages 50 to 60 prospects. These prospects represent the university's most important source of philanthropic support and, quite naturally, command a significant portion of the president's attention. Managing these relationships can be likened to conducting a courtship. The director continuously assesses and consults with other development officers and alumni to determine which gestures would effectively deepen the relationship between each prospect and the university. And as with any courtship, its constant changes requires the director to anticipate, understand, and respond.

In addition to managing these top prospects, the director of principal gifts serves as a consultant to senior development officers in Harvard's academic units and professional schools. These officers may be responsible for principal gift prospects assigned to them on the basis of a specific donor's affiliation or interest. The director also works with senior development officers, deans, and others in the university to develop strategies for the principal gift prospects assigned to the Office of University Capital Giving.

In general, the director's time is divided among three main areas: road work, strategic thinking, and informational and strategic planning meetings:

Road work. In an average week, the director spends one or two days traveling—meeting prospects and volunteers or attending special luncheons or dinners. Although the director seldom asks for gifts directly, developing good strategies for others to do so requires frequent contact with each prospect. This prospect contact sometimes includes discussing gifts, once a solicitation sequence has started, or consulting with donors about about the best strategies for approaching other principal gift prospects. Ideally, such strategies involve the direct participation of donors. The benefits of spending this much time on the road may not be readily apparent in terms of dollars raised from week to week, but over the course of a year or two significant progress in strengthening the generation or likelihood of principal gifts will become evident.

Strategic thinking. Setting aside time away from the distractions of telephones, meetings, and paperwork to think strategically is difficult, but essential. Developing strategies that account for the unique history and qualities of a prospect's relationship with the university requires full and constant attention.

Informational and strategic planning meetings. Evaluating, refining, communicating, and coordinating prospect strategies must be ongoing. Small group meetings to evaluate and refine strategies may include the president, a key volunteer, and fund raisers who have knowledge of specific prospects and can provide fresh perspectives and approaches. At Harvard, larger group meetings bring together from throughout the university those officers or deans who have an interest in the prospects under discussion and serve to communicate and coordinate strategies .

A typical week at Harvard for the director might yield the following schedule:

Monday

Meet with senior development staff for one hour to discuss the coming week's activities. Later, meet with a smaller group of senior fund raisers to develop strategies for principal gift prospects, the agenda of which is managed by the Office of University Capital Giving. This meeting usually includes the vice president and the director of university development, and heads of various units who have knowledge of the prospects or need to know the strategy being developed.

Meet with at least one dean and his or her senior development officer to discuss where the president or a member of the governing board might be helpful with that dean's principal gift prospects. Holding this type of meeting regularly helps coordinate strategy and maintain communication between various units of the university.

Tuesday

Attend meetings similar to Monday's meetings or events in other parts of the university. Monthly, one such meeting brings together the senior development officers from all of the professional schools and the major academic units, along with the vice president and the director of university development. Discussions focus on the progress of principal gift fund raising and strategies regarding the principal gift prospects that the president is scheduled to see next.

Wednesday-Thursday

Meet with prospects. These meetings are conducted as consultations. At Harvard, the director is also the secretary for the Committee on University Resources, which provides a good reason for contacting many influential alumni and friends. But, even without that opening, people in general appreciate being asked for advice. In addition to seeking counsel on prospect strategy or fund-raising planning, the director offers prospects a job to do—writing a letter or setting up a meeting—thereby strengthening a partnership and on-going collaboration.

Late Thursday

Set aside time for planning, strategic thinking, and making use of the information gained during the week.

Friday

Document and disseminate the information gathered from the meetings with prospects and handle the work that has accumulated during the week. Every other Friday, the director meets with the president for one hour to review the strategies and next steps for prospective principal gift donors.

This schedule attempts to reflect the balance that the director must maintain between working inside the university to develop and coordinate prospect strategy and outside the university to gather information and further prospect involvement in the life of the institution.

Staffing the principal gift program

Beyond the director, the principal gift program should have a lean staff: a development associate, an administrative assistant, and a secretary. The lean staff permits the director to limit managerial responsibilities and to focus on fund raising.

At Harvard, the development associate serves as liaison between the Office of University Capital Giving, the academic units, professional schools, and art museums—keeping information on principal gift prospects flowing throughout the University. He or she also gathers information for briefings prepared for the president, and consults with members of various volunteer committees who might have information of value to the principal gift effort.

The administrative assistant provides administrative support; manages a newsletter the office produces for the university's primary development committee, the Committee on University Resources; and handles the logistics for meetings of that committee's executive board.

Conclusion

At a time of increasing competition for philanthropic dollars, the role and importance of large gifts is increasing. Those individuals charged with allocating an institution's development resources may have to focus less on what it would cost to start a principal gift program and focus more on what it is costing to neglect one of the institution's most valuable assets—the talents and resources of its best prospects.

Chapter 11

Developing Prospect Strategies

Marjorie E. Millar
Vice President, (External)
University of Western Ontario
London, Ontario, Canada

D eveloping prospect strategy is one of the most important steps in the major gift process. An investment in time, analysis, and imagination at this stage of the process will maximize the chances of success in asking for and obtaining the major gift. A personalized solicitation tailored to meet the unique needs and interests of an individual prospect is what fund raising is all about.

What is prospect strategy?

Prospect strategy is defined, quite simply, as the approach that a fund raiser takes in order to ask a donor for a gift most appropriately. An individual prospect strategy can be simple, short, and straightforward; it can be complex, long, and subtle. The route you take depends on what you know about the donor, such as the donor's decision-making process, the donor's history of philanthropy, and, most importantly, the donor's motivation to give. Ultimately, matching the donor's motivation to give with your institution's funding priorities will be key to shaping an effective prospect strategy.

Learning about donors and their motivation to give

Understanding donor motivation will help you determine the best way to engage the donor. Do we appeal to the donor's sense of competition or pride? Does the donor want recognition? Does the donor primarily perceive his or her major gift as a rational investment? Does sentiment or a desire to help others motivate the donor the most? The successful major gift fund raiser considers all these questions in developing an effective prospect strategy.

Prospect research files can tell you much about a potential major giver. However, direct contact with the prospective donor is the best vehicle for learning about donor motivation. In fact, the relationship between the prospect and the institution will almost always provide the most comprehensive and effective information regarding the donor's motivation. Development officers, faculty, deans, presidents, and volunteers are all potential parts of this knowledge collection step. Consequently, their input in the prospect strategy process is integral to its success.

As the prospect/institution relationship blossoms, many donors will openly discuss their motivation for giving. Sometimes, fund raisers or other institutional officials may not care for a particular prospective donor's motivation to give, especially when they perceive that the donor's motivation does not match the institution's agenda. In this case, institutional officers may choose to ignore the interests and needs that motivate the donor. A good prospect strategy must face and resolve these issues early in the prospecting stage.

Case statements

Successful major gift fund raising employs some general tools and approaches in developing prospect strategies. One basic prospect strategy tool is the case statement. An effective case statement should:
  • highlight your institution's past accomplishments;
  • delineate the challenges and funding needs that face your institution;
  • outline your plan for meeting these challenges;
  • explain how private support will help your institution; and
  • describe how a prospective donor's gift will play a vital role in your development plan.

The case statement should illustrate that your institution both needs and is worthy of support. Moreover, the case statement should assure each prospective donor that his or her gift *will make a difference*.

When drafting a case statement, you should make sure that the following points are covered as briefly, comprehensively, and competently as possible. Your case statement should tell donors that:
  • we have done great things in the past;
  • we have a track record on which you can rely;
  • we are preparing to do great things in the future;
  • we have an organized plan of action to see this through; and
  • we can do these great things with your help, should your interests coincide with our highest priorities.

Most institutions develop general and specific case statements that describe their overall and specific priority funding needs, respectively. A general case statement conveys an institution's central message to prospective donors. In addition to outlining the needs of the institution as a whole, a general case statement often contains supporting materials such as presentations, videos, and speeches. Moreover, a general case statement sets the stage for the presentation of specific case statements. Specific case statements describe priority funding needs in greater detail, giving the prospective donor an intimate view of a project, activity, or other need.

Whether a case statement is general or specific, it should remind prospective donors that they are associating themselves with your institution's past accomplishments and future achievements.

Understanding donor interest and building involvement

Prospect strategies should use the perceived interests of each donor to match the donor with specific funding priorities. You may wish to enlist the help of volunteers to cultivate, refine, and intensify a donor's interest in and involvement with the life of your institution. Keep in mind, however, that beyond their interest in a particular area of your institution, donors may have another reason or a variety of reasons for making a gift. Keying discussions and proposals to match these reasons can help increase the chances for strong relationships and successful solicitations.

Matching motivation with the gift

One donor may wish to create an enduring monument through a major gift. Another donor may be motivated to give with the idea of establishing a sound investment. Still other donors may intend their gift to make an immediate, positive impact on your institution. In each case, effective prospect strategy will facilitate the donor's desire to choose the type of gift that best reflects his or her motivation.

Endowments. Some donors may wish to keep alive their own name, their family name, or the name of a loved one long after they have gone. One obvious giving choice for these donors is an endowment, which will associate their name with some aspect of the institution in perpetuity. The popularity of endowments should not be underestimated; several endowments at English universities have endured for centuries.

When a donor expresses an interest in establishing an endowment, you should illustrate the permanence of their prospective endowment with examples of other endowments. These examples should feature gifts that have endured for many years, continuously aiding your institution while honoring the donor. Ideally, the example should come from your institution, but if that isn't possible, it is effective to use examples from other institutions.

Facilities. Facilities offer another form of enduring gift. They give donors a chance to connect their names with a tangible and lasting asset that visibly benefits the institution and its students. However, buildings do get torn down. One way to forestall that event is to convince your prospect to fund an endowment for the maintenance and preservation of the facility.

Institutional policies for the naming of facilities should be clear, but flexible. For example, if a building may be named for a gift of 40 percent of the building's cost, your institution may allow donors to contribute this amount through a gift combining endowment and expendable gift funds.

Planned gifts. A donor's estate planning can provide a wonderful opportunity to introduce the topic of deferred gifts. Planned gifts offer donors tax advantages. They also ensure that the donor's gift will continue to play a prominent role in the life of the institution after their death. Depending on the instrument used, planned gifts can make donor assets available to your institution immediately or in the future. Planned gifts also provide the donor with valuable benefits for personal and family financial planning. Continuing stewardship of donors who have made planned gifts provides an excellent opportunity to secure additional gifts during their lifetime.

The full range of planned giving instruments should be considered when deciding prospect strategy. Therefore, it is extremely important that development staff understand various planned giving vehicles and how they work. Fund-raising staff should never urge an agreement or commitment on a donor that would benefit the institution at the expense of the prospect.

Gifts for investment. Some donors consider their gifts to be a form of investment. While most donors want to be assured that their gifts are used wisely, these donors want to know the exact financial details of their gift. Such prospects may want to know how an endowment will be managed. In this case, it is wise to be prepared with facts, charts, and examples of the institution's investment performance. Showing a history of an endowment invested to preserve the buying power of the gift, while also providing a reasonable yield, may be a selling point for investment-minded prospects.

Gifts for immediate impact. Many donors prefer to see the full and immediate impact of their gifts. Such donors may choose to provide expendable support, thereby offering your institution readily available funds. Fully reporting the impact of a gift to the donor can be an effective way to garner further support. A donor may also be interested in establishing an endowment fund that would create an interest pay-out offering the same level of support on an ongoing basis.

Combining endowment and expendable support in a split commitment is a way to offer the donor a gift opportunity with immediate impact, while building a permanent source of future support. In this scenario, the donor may prefer to contribute funds for the naming of a building and an endowment to maintain the continued operation and upgrading of that facility.

Gifts that convey importance. All prospective donors should be made to feel important. However, some donors *need* to feel important—need to know that their gifts are somehow different from or more valued than other gifts.

To meet this need, you may want to take advantage of the timing aspect of a particular fund-raising effort for a priority project. At the beginning of the effort, the prospect appeal can ask for gifts to provide leadership or to "set the pace." As the effort nears its goal, you can urge prospects to offer support to put the project or campaign over the top. Donors may also want to provide mid-campaign support to leverage special matching funds from foundations or the government.

Donors with a special need to feel important may respond well to the idea of funding a challenge grant. Perhaps as a class reunion nears, staff might encourage a prospect to challenge his or her classmates to provide significant reunion gifts. This type of challenge may be particularly attractive to the alumnus or alumna who has achieved success despite the predictions of classmates. Any alumni fund-raising competition must remain friendly and collegial so that the pressure to give does not become uncomfortable or onerous.

Often, the prospect may be part of a community or circle in which large gifts signal the arrival of a certain stature or recognition of success. Here, the promise of publicizing the gift within that community may be the key to a successful solicitation. While recognition is a powerful motivator, it is wise to remember that it has certain inherent dangers.

The role of recognition

Generally, donors do not give just to receive the recognition that a gift generates. Nevertheless, few people can resist the idea of having their generosity publicly and repeatedly acknowledged. Your institution should determine thoughtful recognition policies in advance to guide the activities of major gift officers and volunteers. Such policies will set the stage for recognizing donors in a way that makes everybody happy.

Naming opportunities. Besides scholarship and endowment funds, naming opportunities are a fundamental way of appealing to a donor's desire for recognition. However, unless there are guidelines that chart the different gift sizes with specific levels of name recognition, some donors may feel that they gave too much and received too little. The lack of established guidelines can invite other donors to try to negotiate naming opportunities. You can avoid these pitfalls by establishing clear naming policies.

Gift clubs. Peer recognition is a powerful reward for individual support. To foster peer recognition, your institution may want to establish individual gift clubs for annual giving. Gift clubs formally recognize donors and offer them the opportunity to interact with other major donors at social functions. More importantly, gift clubs "set the pace" for future, larger gifts by giving donors a reason to make significant gifts now. They create an atmosphere that encourages donors to increase their giving toward the level of an ultimate gift.

There are many ways to create a gift club structure. At my institution, we have recently created cumulative gift clubs for recognizing a donor's lifetime commitment. In this way we were able to create a million-dollar recognition vehicle that recognized more than a few members. This kind of gift club lets donors know that their cumulative "megagifts" will be recognized in the future.

Anonymous gifts. Some donors do not want publicity for their gifts; others wish their gifts to be recognized in a private way. Your institution should have a complete non-recognition plan that details the steps you will take to ensure the privacy of donors who wish to remain totally anonymous. It is usually a good idea to assign an account number to totally anonymous gifts, thereby preventing any accidental public listing. Another donor may eschew the public listing of his or her gift, but appreciate a nice thank-you dinner at the president's home.

Reluctant anonymous donors can pose a special challenge to the major gift officer. Such donors profess to want no publicity, but constantly mention all the recognition others are getting. In this case, a gentle discussion with the donor, which reopens the topic of recognition, can go far to preserve the donor/institution relationship.

Creating major gift proposals

After you have learned the donor's interests, motivation, and needs, you should synthesize the prospect strategy for the donor in a personalized major gift proposal. This proposal will:
- identify the prospect's connection to the institution;
- explain why it is important that the donor support a particular project, program, or initiative; and
- show that the donor's gift will be vital to the future of the entire institution. When this proposal is presented to the donor during the solicitation visit, it provides focus and allows the donor to review the case during his or her personal deliberations.

Many of the same qualities that make a good case statement are also the components of a successful major gift proposal. Frantzreb and Pray Associates list the following qualities of a good case statement:[1]

1. Urgency—Why now?
2. Importance—Why does this cause deserve my attention and support?
3. Compassion—Am I moved by this? Does it have heart as well as mind?
4. Credibility—Can this institution do what it says it will?
5. Positiveness—Are they confident, upbeat?
6. Readability—Is it all esoteric prose, or do I understand?
7. Concreteness—Are there facts I can get hold of and objects that I can measure?

What makes an excellent proposal is a matter of judgment. No single format or style guarantees success. Length is not as important as the proposal's ability to answer the questions listed above and to address directly the donor's needs and motivation.

Conclusion

No one questions the importance of a major gift effort for educational fund raising. However, as institutions are facing ever-diminishing budgets, many administrators are adopting an increasingly short-term view of fund raising. "We need the money now" is the political view that sometimes dominates major gift efforts. Development professionals need to exercise a long-term view in order to foster successful major gift fund raising. It naturally follows that the development of prospect strategies should incorporate this long-term view as well. When prospect strategy has been set—taking into account the university's priorities, the prospect's priorities, the fit and motivation—the right time will present itself for a successful ask.

And finally, when the institution's professional team and its trusted volunteers set guidelines, expect that there always will be exceptions. Experience will help show when and how to deal with an unusual situation. The best major gift strategists are the most-informed and flexible ones.

Notes

[1] Frantzreb and Pray Associates, Inc. "The Case Statement as a Factor of Institutional Management and Development."

Chapter 12

Factors of Engagement: Using Volunteer Committees And Special Events to Cultivate Donors

Charlotte B. Heartt
Director of Development
Smith College
Northampton, Massachusetts

G ood cultivation is essential to the success of any fund-raising program, not only because it stimulates the potential donor's interest and awareness, but also because it strengthens the personal connection between donor and institution. Both ingredients are essential to successful solicitation and the long-term growth of a development effort.

Personalized correspondence and printed materials, (newsletters, brochures, alumni and alumnae magazines, etc.) are good methods of cultivating donors. Such materials convey to the prospect a clear sense of the institution's mission and activities. During the early stages of cultivation, factual information helps to build awareness by giving the donor tangible evidence of your institution's history and goals. To be truly effective in leading a donor to commitment, you will need to employ a more personal touch, such as visits with a trustee, president, or other institutional representative. As donor cultivation moves into later and more intimate stages, special events and volunteer committees encourage prospects to cement their involvement with your institution by providing a major gift or other support.

Using special events to involve donors

The cultivation of prospects through special events is effective because these events provide:
- a link between your institution's past and present activities;
- an opportunity for prospects to meet the president, trustees, and other key members of the administration;
- a chance for donors to meet one another and create informal networks; and
- a source of pride and positive association with your institution.

On-campus events. Because they ease coordination and provide direct campus experience, on-campus events are among the most common and effective means of cultivating alumni prospects. They can also offer prospects who are not alumni a wonderful opportunity to gather positive impressions of your institution.

The simplest on-campus event to plan is one that coincides with a planned ceremony on campus. The dedication of a building or other campus landmark is a good opportunity for cultivation and stewardship. Such on-campus events bring to life the adage, "nothing succeeds like success." In celebrating a completed building or renovation project, the formal naming of a chaired professor, or the installation of artwork or technology, the institution's success is apparent to potential donors, most of whom prefer to contribute to a successful organization.

At Smith College we marked the conclusion of a successful campaign by dedicating a new science center. Donors, dignitaries, and faculty received attractive invitations announcing the dedication and explaining its importance to the campaign and the college. At the dedication, prospects joined with donors, faculty, and local dignitaries to share in this important accomplishment. The event both thanked the donors for their support and instilled in them the sense that the college was indeed worthy of their future support.

On-campus visits. Many institutions invite prospects and their spouses or guests to campus for weekend visits. On-campus visits encourage alumni to feel nostalgic for the college they knew and loved in the past, while noting its current growth and development. They also help nonalumni prospects to "get a feel" for your institution and its special needs. The goal of the weekend is to provide a unified, coherent message from a strong and welcoming academic institution.

Weekend visits give alumni and other prospects a chance to acquaint themselves with your institution to a greater degree than they could through a single event. The greater length of time on campus and the fact that most guests stay overnight at the same lodging provide opportunities for cultivation and mutual involvement. On-campus weekends allow guests to: socialize with peers and staff; attend the institution's cultural events; visit classes; meet faculty; and hear presentations from key administrators regarding the state of the institution. The combination of events helps alumni feel like "insiders" again and has the added benefit of giving nonalumni their own association with your institution. Another lasting effect of the weekend visit is that participants develop informal networks that endure long after the visit.

Weekend visits allow the trustees, president, and development staff to get to know the prospect group better. Later in the cultivation process, this kind of personal knowledge often results in better cultivation and solicitation strategies. Moreover, during such visits prospects can meet in confidence with development officers to discuss the important details of their giving plans, questions about specific giving opportunities, and other "nuts and bolts" of making a major gift.

Often, a volunteer group of your institution may wish to sponsor a weekend visit to campus. If this is the case, volunteers should work closely with staff before the event to ensure smooth coordination of on-campus personnel and facilities once guests arrive. Volunteers and staff should inform the president, trustees, and deans of any special individual prospects attending the weekend visit and their particular areas of interest. Often guests request appointments with faculty or staff representitives to discuss a particular project.

Off-campus events. Whether they occur on or off campus, special events are extremely effective cultivation tools. However, off-campus events offer two additional cultivation opportunities that their on-campus counterparts do not:

- the chance to attract a wider audience drawn from friends and prospects who do not or cannot travel back to campus; and
- a sense among alumni that their institution has appeal and attention outside its own location.

For potential donors who are concerned that your institution is too "insular," off-campus events can be a means of convincing them that your institution has broad impact and is worthy of support.

Off-campus events require the thorough coordination of development staff, institutional leadership, and volunteers. Therefore, make it a priority to devote appropriate staff, time, and resources to the planning and execution of your off-campus events. Careful attention to "up-front" details will be your best recipe for encouraging donors and prospects to attend your event. If possible, garner as much media coverage in the local market where the off-campus event will take place.

Promoting involvement through volunteer committees

Involving special prospects in the volunteer "workforce" increases their knowledge and understanding of the institution's programs, deepens their affiliation, and encourages their philanthropy. Generally, institutions with successful fund-raising programs have a history of volunteer involvement in their external relations programs.

This is certainly true at Smith College. For over a decade, Smith has mobilized alumnae and parents both here and abroad to advance its development efforts. Volunteer committees support both capital campaigns and annual fund raising. During campaigns, lead donors form soliciting committees to cultivate campaign prospects. Non-soliciting networking committees support capital efforts between campaigns. Additionally, volunteer networks and advisory groups act in a consulting capacity to several departments and offices on campus.

Development staff train and support volunteers in every phase of their work throughout their committee terms. Volunteers participate in cultivation/solicitation training meetings at least once where they learn about the college's programs. In addition, the meetings help volunteers to generate their own interest and enthusiasm for current fund-raising efforts.

A typical training program lasts one day, includes a working lunch, and features a presentation on fund-raising techniques by a consultant. Training days occur either before or after a special event, to which the spouses or guests of volunteers are invited. In this way, volunteers receive technical fund-raising information combined with an emotional component—a revitalized feeling for the campus and its students. Without exception, volunteers leave with:

- a renewed commitment to the institution;
- a sense of pride in serving with an impressive group of peers; and
- a feeling of excitement for the challenging work that lies ahead.

Outreach to potential donors is virtually unlimited through such a volunteer committee structure. During the $152-million Campaign for Smith, more than 100 alumnae and parent couples assisted the solicitations of more than 600 major donor prospects. These were special prospects with a giving potential in the $100,000- to $1-million range. This volunteer effort resulted in a campaign that totaled more than $163 million in gifts. The personal generosity of volunteers during the campaign was extraordinary. Many volunteers made their largest commitments ever, and also pledged additional gifts toward the end of the five-and-a-half-year effort. In addition to substantially increasing Smith's support, this remarkable rally on the college's behalf dispelled, at last, the myth that only men make large gifts.

Keeping institutional/donor relationships personal and satisfying

Ultimately, the relationship that the institution builds with an individual donor will determine the level of support that donor is willing to give. As a general rule, donors will not make a major commitment until they feel a direct sense of personal involvement with your institution. Therefore, it is vitally important to give prospects and donors many opportunities to involve themselves with your institution in a gratifying way.

Most colleges and universities report that they receive their largest campaign gifts from donors who are most involved with their institution. This includes donors who were trustees or key volunteers, attended cultivation programs, or who were actively cultivated in other ways over the years by a trustee, volunteer, or other college representative.

Personal donor involvement can offer other kinds of fund-raising support to your institution. For example, a Smith trustee who was somewhat reluctant to vote in favor of a capital campaign because she wasn't convinced it would succeed, managed through a personal cultivation visit to secure one of the campaign's largest gifts. She had visited a widower many years before to talk to him from the heart about what Smith had meant to her. He was so affected by her presentation that he left his entire estate to Smith when he died a few years later. With the announcement of this bequest, the trustee became one of the strongest campaign supporters on the board.

Conclusion

With constant cultivation, the relationships built with donors before and during a campaign can continue to grow and flourish after that special effort is over. Though you may need to make initial investments of extra patience and persistence, these relationships can strengthen a fund-raising program for years to come.

Chapter 13

Asking for Major Gifts

A. H. "Bud" Edwards
Vice Chancellor for University Advancement
University of Arkansas
Fayetteville, Arkansas

William Outhouse
Director of Development
University of Arkansas
Fayetteville, Arkansas

You've got to ask

When I was in college back in the early 1950s, I had a friend, Ken, who somehow managed to get a date every single time he wanted one. Whether it was Friday night at the movies, Saturday at the ball game, Sunday at church, or some other special occasion, Ken would always be there with a date. Because I was never that lucky, it was difficult for me to understand how he could be so successful on such a consistent basis. I finally had to ask:

"Ken, how come you're never without a date?"

"I guess it's because I always ask," he replied.

"Yeah, but it seems like you never get turned down," I persisted.

"Oh, I get turned down a lot," he responded. "I just keep asking. Sometimes I have to ask 10 different people before I find one who will say 'yes.' Also, I often have to ask the same one several times before she says 'yes.'"

This lesson in dating also can be a first lesson in fund raising. You've got to ask for the money in order to receive the money.

It taught me the importance of setting *asking goals*. There may be times I will have to ask 10 different people in order to get one "yes." I simply won't get a gift every time I ask. And I've come to understand another important lesson:

although the same prospect may say "no" to a particular request, this does not necessarily mean this prospect will say "no" to every future request.

In fund raising, you can bet that if you don't ask, you stand a 100 percent chance of not getting a gift. And, even when you do ask, there are times you will get turned down. To succeed you will need to analyze why your prospect said no, and then begin preparing to ask again.

Does it make any difference who asks?

While there is no argument that you have to ask for a major gift in order to get one, there is a lot of discussion and debate over just who should do the asking.

Some people will argue that no one but a peer volunteer is qualified to do the asking. Others dispute this point of view. They say that the president of the institution or someone from the development staff should do the asking, because they are better trained.

Both sides can cite stories to back up their arguments and both may be correct. There is, however, also reason to believe that volunteers, development staff, presidents, and deans are equally important to the successful solicitation of a gift. Taken together, they constitute a three-person team, each individual bringing his or her own special strengths to the solicitation process:

Volunteers:
1. They are peers and are held in high regard by the business community in general and the prospective donor in particular.
2. They have made a major gift.
3. They have knowledge of and a long-term association with your institution.
4. They believe in the project for which you are soliciting a gift.
5. They aren't paid to say what they do.

Development staff:
1. They have a long-term association with the prospect.
2. They are good listeners.
3. They have the ability to staff the solicitation team.
4. If necessary, they can ask for the gift.
5. They can write accurate call reports.
6. They can work with urgency on appropriate follow-up.

Presidents and deans:
1. They are good presenters.
2. They can ask for the gift.
3. They can commit the institution to the project for which you are soliciting funds.
4. They can be flexible with a donor's needs.

Though the development officer seldom asks for the gift under this three-person approach, he or she does play a crucial role in the solicitation process. It is the role of the development officer to:
- schedule and conduct briefings and training sessions for the team;
- see that meeting dates are set with the prospective donor; and
- guide the project along a workable time schedule.

Because this is a difficult job, the wise use of time and other resources is essential.

In addition to being the solicitation organizer, the development officer must also be something of an expert in human relations. The development officer must be able to request and receive the best work of everyone involved in the solicitation. Often, the most difficult part of this task is finding ways to work effectively with the president, the dean, or another institutional official. When this is the case, treat these individuals the same way you would treat a donor; make your points tactfully and don't argue. This approach will help you overcome road blocks and keep your emotional balance.

Many factors can affect a successful solicitation. The make up of the solicitation team and how well that team is staffed are two of the most important factors for positive results.

The time line, board members, and other factors for closing the gift

One of the first questions the president of any institution always asks is: "How soon can we expect our first major gift?"

The answer to this question is quite clear: it depends.

The time line. Closing a major gift generally takes anywhere from one month to two years. If a prospective donor has been closely associated with your institution for two or more years, you could close a major gift with that prospect in as little as one month. If a prospect has not been involved in the life of your institution, it could take up to 24 months to close a major gift. Some major gifts will require a lifetime of good relationships before you will see any results.

Board members. Cultivating the involvement of your board and other key volunteers in fund-raising activities is an important factor in moving major gifts to closure. If your institution is going to be involved in major gift fund raising, you need to have capable leadership on your board of trustees and other key advisory boards. Your boards should include people who can make a major "lead" gift and help you close other major gifts. You will need the influence of these strong volunteers. Maintain ongoing dialogues with board members and other key volunteers about how your institution can meet the needs of major donor prospects. These dialogues should make up a significant part of any staff person's time.

Targeting and expressing donor needs. You must define what the gift will do for the donor in an insightful and appealing way. Donors do not give major gifts because your institution needs the money. They give them because of their own needs. The sooner you can identify the donor's needs, the sooner you will be able to close a gift. This is one reason we spend so much time cultivating the prospective donor. The longer the time we spend building relationships and getting to know prospects, the shorter the time it will take to close the gift.

When it comes to planning a major gift solicitation, if a development officer is thinking about anything other than how a gift can benefit the donor, he or she is probably thinking about the wrong thing.

Keep your eye on the prospect. One fact always holds true in major gift fund raising: you can only get money from people who have money. The more people you have associated with your institution who have affluence and influence, the better your chances will be of successfully soliciting and closing major gifts. Building relationships with people of affluence and influence should be the number one priority for the development staff of any institution. When analyzing the ability of an institution to close major gifts, assessing the number of monied prospects involved in the life of the institution is probably the most important factor one can consider.

Tools to guide the ask

The development staff should work with *urgency*. Urgency is an internal force that motivates us to action. It is a self-insistence of purpose that stays with us until we meet all of our objectives. With urgency, we take on an importunate attitude; that is, we refuse to be denied. This attitude will help us "drive home" the major gift.

Resources. The development staff should skillfully utilize all its resources. A resource is anything that lies ready for us to use in our quest to accomplish goals. These resources may include time invested, budget, volunteers, personnel, or facilities. The likelihood of success increases when we use our resources prudently and effectively. We must also use our resources properly to deal promptly with problems and difficulties that may arise and interfere with our ability to reach our goals and objectives.

Responsiveness. The development staff should be responsive. Responsiveness means communicating accurately and readily when a prospective donor makes a suggestion, asks a question, or requests information. It means working with a sense of urgency when dealing with prospective donors, volunteers, board members, and members of the faculty and staff. A quick and accurate response to a donor's request will increase the confidence, respect, and support of that person for both the development officer and the institution.

Luck. A little bit of luck always helps, too. Luck is the seemingly chance happening of events that affect our fortune. We can, however, influence our luck. Working with *urgency*, using our *resources* wisely, and *responding* quickly and accurately to prospective donors, volunteers, and faculty have a wonderful way of increasing our good luck. Doing the right thing, in the right place, at the right time increases our results.

Results are what we get from working with urgency, resources, responsiveness, and luck. These results may include an increase in major gifts, the addition or retention of key volunteers, or a better working relationship with other college or university personnel.

Putting it all together. How do you know if you are working with a sense of urgency? Are you being resourceful? Are you being responsive? The following checklist of key action points might be a good indicator:

1. Do you have a plan and are you following it?
2. Are you thinking about your major gift prospects every day?
3. Do you believe in your mission and are you practicing it?
4. Are you cultivating people who can give you a major gift? (Remember: you can only get money from people who have it.)
5. Are you doing "right" things? (Do "right" things; even if you don't do them "right," you will be successful.)
6. Are you involving people of influence and affluence with your institution

over a long period of time?

7. Are you managing up as well as down? (Are you coordinating the president, the dean, and staff?)

8. Are you doing the hard things first, every day?

9. Do you set asking goals?

10. Do you set objectives when you have an event?

11. When you only have time to do one thing, are you seeing a prospect?

12. Are you building relationships with internal constituents?

13. Are you listening more and talking less?

14. Do you feel your case and do you share that feeling?

15. Are you having fun? Do you enjoy your job?

Setting the stage for the solicitation meeting

Using the right approach. There are two commonly used approaches to asking a prospective donor for a major gift. One is to prepare a proposal, put together a solicitation team, set a meeting, and go ask. This is the approach you should use when you are certain of the donor's interest and giving potential.

When you are unsure of these two pieces of information, it's time to try a second approach. In this case, you should:

• put together a preliminary team that can talk with the prospective donor comfortably and effectively:

• set a meeting; and

• go ask the prospect if he or she would be willing to entertain a proposal for a gift.

During that meeting, discuss the prospect's interests and the level of his or her giving potential. Once you have learned the prospect's motivation, structure your proposal, put together a solicitation team, set another meeting, and go ask for the gift.

The value of this two-step approach in soliciting a major gift cannot be overstated. Not long ago the major gift officer from our college of business invited me to go on just such a call. We met with one of the college's successful graduates whom was now the head of a large nursing home chain. The prospect had been carefully cultivated for more than two years, had a good relationship with both the dean of the college and the chancellor of the university, and certainly had the capability of making a large gift. Only the specific interests of the prospect remained unclear.

We had three objectives that we wanted to accomplish during our meeting with him. Our first objective was to find out if he and his company would entertain a major gift proposal. The second objective was to determine the appropriate amount to ask for in our proposal. And our third objective was to learn more specifically the prospect's interests. Was he interested in endowing a named scholarship? Was he interested in faculty development? Was he interested in supporting a particular department or program? We just weren't certain.

In just one hour we were able to achieve all three objectives. The results were surprising. First, the prospect was most receptive to our asking for a gift. Second, based on the company's past giving record, a gift in the $500,000 range was probably the highest this prospect could stretch. And third, the prospect's greatest interest was where the university's nursing program was housed, not in the college of business, but in the college of education. This was the first time he had ever mentioned nursing as his key interest to anyone at the university.

While this information caused some consternation for the major gift officer at the college of business, it was vital to the ultimate success of our solicitation. If we hadn't taken the time for this preliminary meeting, we would have missed vital information, and we would not have been successful in closing the gift.

Setting the tone. Whether your solicitation process covers one or two meetings, it is important that you set the tone for what is going to happen. Before you arrive, you should let the prospect know that this will not be an ordinary meeting. Your team is there to discuss some very urgent and important issues.

The words and phrases you use in making the appointment and conducting the meeting set the tone. Let the donor know that you consider him or her to be very special. Frame the project you want to talk about in a vital and exciting way. There are many words and phrases you could use to convey these messages. Here are just a few:

> "Only a few people can make a difference and you are one of them."
> "We need your support if we are to realize this dream that we both share."
> "Wouldn't it be wonderful if ...."
> "One of your dreams can be realized."
> "When we talked some time ago, you gave us this really great idea. Let me tell you what we've come up with as a result."

Understanding donor motivation. There are many theories on what motivates a donor to make a gift. We operate under the theory that all donors carry around a kind of "pain" inside themselves. This pain comes from feelings of guilt, discomfort, anxiety, indebtedness, or frustration that for which they have been unable to find an outlet or release. When you ask a donor for the gift, you offer the donor an opportunity to relieve some of his or her pain. You are a kind of broker between the donor's pain (need) and your institution's pain (need).

Begin to involve the donor in a discussion of his or her pain as early as possible. This discussion could begin months or years before the solicitation meeting. Whatever the time line, you will need to understand the donor's pain absolutely. Only then will you be able to show the donor how he or she can relieve that pain by investing in one of your programs.

The solicitation meeting: Closing the gift

These basic steps will help you conduct your solicitation meeting. You may break the steps down differently than we have here, or call them by other names. What is important is that you include all the steps and carry them out in sequence. We call the steps *greeting, questioning, listening, presenting the proposal, overcoming objections*, and *asking for the gift*.

Greeting. The greetings you exchange with the donor during the meeting's first three to five minutes may be the most important part of your time together. From the very beginning, you must bring a sense of excitement about why you are there. At the same time, you must involve the prospect in the conversation. It is important that the prospect begin to relate to you on a personal level during those first few minutes. Find common ground. Talk about football, family, children, music, common friends, an award, or other honor recently received by the prospect; talk about anything that will help you and the prospect relate on a person-to-person level. Be sincere as you do this, however, or the prospect will see through you before the first minute goes by.

Wherever you meet (in the prospect's office, in his or her home, in a meeting room, or in a restaurant), the spokesperson for your team should sit where he or she can maintain eye contact with the prospect. Try to keep distractions to a minimum. The solicitation spokesperson should always be confident, maintain a positive attitude, and keep the focus of the conversation on the prospect.

After the greetings have taken place, the solicitation spokesperson should begin to look for a way to direct the conversation toward the purpose at hand. One of the best ways to accomplish this is to ask an attention-getting question. Suppose, for example, that your prospect is the widow of a noted research engineer. The purpose of your visit is to solicit her late husband's vast library of papers. You also seek funds to process and catalog the holdings, so that they can be used by other researchers at the university. You might begin the questioning phase of the solicitation by asking the following question:

> "Mrs. Giffels, I know that you have some real concerns about what is going to happen to your husband's research papers. Perhaps, the university can be of some help in this matter. Would you mind if I ask you a few questions about his papers?"

Besides keeping the prospect involved, this type of question will lead both of you into the questioning part of the meeting.

Questioning. The best way to move the conversation toward the solicitation is to ask open-ended questions that allow your prospect to do most of the talking. The right kinds of questions will encourage the prospect to talk about his or her pain and reconfirm your own thinking about the prospect's interests and needs. Your questioning may also uncover any reservations or doubts that the prospect may have, which you may not have known about before.

Your objective is to elicit answers from the donor that contain force and feeling. Keep the questions short and the answers long. Spend lots of staff time going over questions before you go to the meeting. Asking the right questions will help you to: control the meeting; challenge the prospect; keep the meeting on track; and enable the prospect to feel the "pain" of what is and what can be. Later you will help the donor to see a possible solution for releasing this "pain."

Listening. Listening is a difficult skill to master, but it's one that every development officer should learn. Most people speak at one-fourth the speed that their brain is able to comprehend. This gives us a lot of time to hear what the prospect is saying and to formulate our next question or comment.

Listening is an active, selective, and participatory process. Listen with your ears and eyes. Be responsive. Nod or smile from time to time to give visible feedback. Show your prospect that you are listening to his or her every word. At the proper time, summarize for the prospect what you have heard him or her say. Then, present your proposal and explain the ways it can benefit the donor's wishes.

Presenting the proposal. Although you can present your proposal verbally, experience shows that a written proposal lends weight to your solicitation. Always bring a written proposal to the solicitation to leave with your prospect. While the written proposal can be as long as 40 or 50 pages, most of the time it is no longer than two or three pages. Even $1-million proposals don't have to be long.

The written proposal should focus on the prospective donor and his or her interests and accomplishments in words that are warm and personal. It should describe the prospect's "pain" and how you propose to ease or alleviate that "pain," again in words that convey feeling and sincerity. Only after the first two points are covered, should the proposal explain the program or activity you want the prospect to support.

As you present your proposal, it is important to use words and phrases like:
- "We have an idea we'd like to present to you for your consideration"; or
- "We have an idea that we believe is both interesting and exciting. We'd like to present it to you and get your opinion."

Remember that you are just asking the prospect to hear you out and to keep an open mind. You will make the specific "ask" later in the solicitation.

Share your views with the prospect. Explain that you feel the proposal outlines the best way to meet his or her need. Add that an investment in this project will guarantee its success now and far into the future. Share stories about gifts of other donors that relate to the prospect's point of view. Tell how others have solved their problems and alleviated their "pain" through investing in your institution.

At this point, it is important to ask questions that keep the prospect involved in the solicitation process. Though you are putting forth ideas, you are also looking for reactions that show whether you are on track with the prospect. If you get positive, interested feedback from the donor, you should proceed. If you don't, you might want to consider withdrawing your proposal. Then, suggest to the prospect that, based on what you have learned through this conversation, you want to go back and rework your proposal. Assure the prospect that you wish to visit further about the new proposal at some later date.

Overcoming objections. If your prospect has any reluctance to your proposal at all, it will generally come out during this part of the solicitation meeting. Do not be surprised or upset if it does. The decision to give away a large sum of money is seldom simple. As the reluctance or objections surface, assure the prospect that your institution can and will meet his or her needs. Never be defensive. By raising objections to your proposal or stalling for more time when more time is not the real problem, the prospect is not attacking you. Rather, the prospect may just be looking for assurance that accepting your proposal is the right thing to do. Only the prospect can decide that. However, you can help by being understanding and by telling the prospect about how others have made similar gifts that changed or influenced their lives.

Never argue or dispute your prospect's objections. Remember, your prospect is always right no matter what you think. You will never get a major gift by trying to prove your prospect wrong. Always show him or her that you appreciate and understand the importance of these objections. Take time to explore the prospect's objections with care and concern. Then move on to asking for the gift.

Asking for the gift. After you have presented and discussed the proposal, it is time for the spokesperson of your solicitation team to ask for the gift. For some, the ask is the most difficult part of the solicitation meeting. It is also the most important part of the process. If you don't ask, you stand a 100 percent chance of not getting the gift. If you do ask, your chances are at least 50-50.

There are ways to make the ask easier. Rather than ask point blank, "Will you make this gift?" you might try a softer, more indirect approach like:

> "Mr./Ms. Prospect, we want you to know that in asking you to fund this project, we don't expect you to make the entire gift all at once. If you would like, you may spread your gift over the next three to five years and even longer. Because the project is vitally important to our university, we will be happy to help you explore the gift possibility that best fits your needs. Would a long-term gift work better for you?"

After you ask for the gift, be quiet. Do not try to help the prospect make his or her decision. No matter how long it takes, after you ask for the gift, let your prospect be the next to speak. If you speak first, it is probably because you are nervous about the amount of the gift. Your natural tendency will be to let the donor know that if he or she wishes to make a smaller gift, you will understand. Do not make this mistake. Let your prospect make that decision.

Sometimes you will get exactly what you ask for; most of the time you will need to negotiate. When negotiating with a prospect, follow the most positive course of discussion. You shouldn't talk about whether the donor will make the gift. Rather, encourage the donor to discuss the size of his or her gift, the number of years required to pay out the gift, or whether it will be a guaranteed or a deferred gift.

When your prospect agrees to the gift, give your new donor support through congratulations and expressions of sincere gratitude.

The memorandum of understanding

Now that your prospect has become a major gift donor, it is a good idea to prepare a memorandum of understanding. A memorandum of understanding describes exactly the donor's intention for the gift. It also outlines the responsibility and role of the institution in managing the donor's gift. Gifts that establish a permanent endowment fund or underwrite a program that would extend over several years, require a memorandum of understanding.

The memorandum of understanding is the first step in the stewardship of the gift. It helps the donor feel secure that the gift will be used according to his or her wishes. In addition, the memorandum will help the administrators of the gift to know exactly what the donor wants without having to rely on memory. The memorandum "heads off at the pass" any future confusion on the part of the donor and the institution.

Please note that a memorandum of understanding is just what its name implies: it is a written understanding of the donor's intention for the gift and a written commitment of how the institution will care for the gift. Despite its appearance, a memorandum of understanding is not, by itself, a legal document.

We have included a model memorandum of understanding for establishing an endowment fund on page 107 (Figure 13-1). You can adjust the model to fit the needs of nearly any institution or gift.

The next appointment

If possible, set the next appointment date before you leave the solicitation meeting. Explain that you would like to bring back a draft memorandum of understanding for the donor's review. Once approved, you will prepare a final memorandum of understanding for the donor's signature and yours.

An unhappy ending?

What if you don't need a memorandum? What if you need Maalox? What if, despite your best efforts, your prospect turns down your proposal? Relax. If your proposal was presented with confidence in your cause and consideration for your prospective donor, even a "no" can be a step forward. A thoughtful ask, which is tailored to the donor's interests, will cause your donor to give your future proposals careful consideration.

Remember, in most cases, a solicitation is not the end of the relationship, but part of the relationship. Don't focus on "no"; focus on tomorrow and just keep asking. It works.

Figure 13-1: Model memorandum of understanding to establish an endowment fund

Note: the information in **bold** will vary depending on the nature of the gift and the details of agreement.

It is the expressed wish of **William and Mary Smith** to establish an Endowed Fund to **provide an annual scholarship at Your Institution in memory of their late son, William Smith Jr. This scholarship will be awarded to an outstanding student desiring to major in English.**

The following are the terms and conditions for the establishment of the Endowment Fund and **for the scholarship to be supported by its income:**

1. NAME: The name of the Endowment Fund shall be the **William Smith Jr. Endowed Scholarship Fund.**

2. FUNDING: For purposes of establishing the Fund, **William and Mary Smith** intend to deposit **$50,000** in Your Institution Foundation, Inc. in amounts of not less than **$10,000 annually**, beginning **December ___, 1993**. The Fund shall be an open fund, capable of receiving additional contributions at any time.

Funds invested in the **William Smith Jr. Endowed Scholarship Fund** shall be managed by Your Institution Foundation, Inc., under guidelines established and reviewed annually by the Board of Directors of Your Institution Foundation, Inc. Unexpended earnings shall be added to the principal. At no time shall Endowment principal be expended.

3. PURPOSE: The purpose of the **William Smith Jr. Endowed Scholarship Fund** shall be to **support annually a scholarship for an undergraduate student in English, to be selected by the appropriate academic faculty**.

4. RECOGNITION, PROMOTION, ACKNOWLEDGMENT, and REPORTING: In order to honor the **memory of William Smith Jr.**, express the appreciation of **Your Institution** to **William and Mary Smith**, enhance the **William Smith Jr. Endowed Scholarship Fund**, and attract gifts for similar purposes, it is understood that appropriate publicity in the form of announcements to news media, internal and external publications, and other suitable recognition may be made by **Your Institution** and **Your Institution Foundation, Inc.**

Annually, the **Appropriate Academic Department** shall report to the donor(s) regarding disbursement of funds and the recipients of the funds.

5. ADMINISTRATION: Selection of the recipient(s) of the **William Smith Jr. Scholarship** shall be the responsibility of the _____ under the supervision of the _____ at **Your Institution**. (Insert the name of the person or committee responsible for administering the gift.)

6. CHANGED CONDITIONS: If, in the future, circumstances have so altered that it is no longer feasible, in the opinion of the Board of Directors of **Your Institution**, to continue the terms of this agreement, said Board of Directors shall be required to apply this fund to such purposes as may, in its opinion, most closely fulfill the intentions of the donors herein described.

7. FORMAL ACCEPTANCE: All signatories to this document shall, in good faith, carry out the terms and conditions of this gift as spelled out in items one through seven of this Memorandum of Understanding and shall do so to the best of their ability. The terms and conditions of this Memorandum of Understanding shall become binding on the institution only after it is presented to **Your Institution** Board of Directors for proper action and acceptance, after which a signed copy of board action shall be presented to the donor.

Donor Signatures
Accepting Memorandum
of Agreement:

Institutional Signatures
Accepting Memorandum
of Agreement:

_____

Donor

_____

President
Vice President
Director of Development
(any of above are acceptable)

_____

Donor

_____

Dean or Chair of Appropriate
Department

(You can add more signatures as needed.)

Chapter 14

Major Gift Case Studies

James W. Osterholt
Assistant Vice Chancellor-Development

Roger A. Meyer
Associate Director of University Development
Major Gift Programs
University of California, Los Angeles
Los Angeles, California

S ecuring major gifts involves a series of organized activities dealing with the identification, cultivation, and solicitation of potential donors. Many of these activities require very specific professional, technical, and informational expertise and processes.

At its heart, however, successful major gift fund raising is a personal process of establishing and building relationships. This "personal touch" can be as elusive as it is valuable; it is the critical part of fund raising that cannot be quantified or fit into any of the boxes of a tracking database. Nevertheless, there are certain "basics" to establishing personal relationships with donors that lend themselves to definition. These basics include, but are not restricted to, the following points:

• development staff must always recognize that donors make gifts because they believe in an institution;

• development staff must always recognize that donors make gifts because they have a positive and satisfying relationship with an institution;

• donors will make major gifts only after they are engaged and involved;

• donors make gifts based upon their interest in and involvement with people, who can include development staff, the president, institutional leaders, board members, and faculty;

• personal relationships always play an important role in each donor's decision-making process about gifts;

• because donors want to see the results of their philanthropy, it is critical that staff provide continued attention to the quality of donor relationships.

When development officers and institutional leaders remember the "basics," productive relationships result in increased support. When we forget those basic guidelines, our efforts fail.

Although the basics may seem straightforward, it is impossible to state precisely how they shape a meaningful major donor relationship. Therefore, we turned to past experience to describe how the basics work. Although these case studies are representative of actual cases, they are in fact compilations of various discussions and events.

The following case studies illustrate how building major donor relationships can succeed or fail in securing private support. In doing so, these cases help to remind us of the importance of keeping the basics in mind. It is also important to keep in mind that creating the relationships described here required time and patience. When reading the condensed version of these events, remember that what takes a minute to narrate took years to build.

The Johnson family

Scenario. The Johnson family members were longtime friends and supporters of our institution. A campus landmark bore their name, and Mr. Johnson had been a leading volunteer in our development program. Throughout their years of involvement, they had consistently made gifts that supported our highest priorities. Specifically, the Johnsons had shown a particular fondness for projects that helped students.

Mr. Johnson was a leader of our last campaign, to which he made a generous gift. During the campaign, Mr. and Mrs. Johnson also became acquainted with our university's chancellor. This acquaintance grew into a close, personal relationship between the Johnsons and the chancellor. Development staff helped this relationship along through their stewardship activities surrounding the Johnson's campaign gift.

As the campaign's final year approached, we realized that we were approaching our campaign goal, and would likely exceed it. Despite this overall success, we were concerned that the campaign would not meet one of its most critical objectives, student support. With these circumstances in mind, we began to consider how we might use the final year of the campaign to focus on securing gifts for student support, while at the same time celebrating the overall success of the campaign.

These deliberations led the chancellor to ask Mr. and Mrs. Johnson for a multi-million challenge grant to encourage other donors to make gifts for scholarships and fellowships. We assured the Johnsons that their gift would "take us over the top," as well as focus the final year's activities on achieving one of our most important objectives.

The Johnsons were pleased with our proposal and provided their major gift. When we received the gift, we used the gift's announcement to launch a challenge campaign. Moreover, we were able to acknowledge publicly that we had reached our published goal exactly one year early.

The gift energized our volunteer leadership just at the point of the inevitable "end of campaign letdown," and strengthened the focus of our last campaign year. The faculty was pleased that the gift would provide support for students and enhance the quality of the students they would teach.

Lessons learned. Why was our request received so favorably? How did our relationship with the Johnsons help to bring about this major gift?

First, we were successful because we recognized the importance of our relationship with the Johnsons, including its cause and history. The Johnsons had always wanted to help our institution where our needs were the greatest. In addition, they were particularly intent on helping students.

Second, we were able to appeal to the Johnsons based on the relationship that they had shared with our institution. When we requested their support, we were able to do so in the spirit of a mutual effort: the the Johnsons would help us to ensure the campaign's success, as well as increase student support .

Finally, and most importantly, we remembered that relationships are the basis of gift giving. Knowing this, we chose that the chancellor make the request of the Johnsons for major gift support. In summary, we remembered the "basics."

Mrs. Gordon

Scenario. Mr. and Mrs. Gordon were longtime supporters of the arts. Mr. Gordon was an artist by training, and he and his wife enjoyed many relationships across the visual and performing arts spectrum. They took great pleasure in supporting the artistic work of their friends. This meant that they made a large number of what might be termed "special" gifts, rather than concentrating their support in a smaller number of major gifts. The Gordons often spoke of the joy they received from seeing the results of their gifts "sprout" in many different places.

Given this history and consistent pattern of giving, it was somewhat surprising when the Gordons approached us with the idea of establishing an award program at our institution. They intended the proposed award program to be a "Nobel for Art." The Gordons wanted to fund the program on an annual basis, and guarantee it in perpetuity through their estates. Sadly, Mr. Gordon died shortly after proposing this gift. His passing ended discussion of the award program.

Two years later, Mrs. Gordon informed us that she wanted to endow the program in her husband's memory. She requested that we prepare a proposal stating how we would administer the program, and the criteria by which we would propose to make the awards.

What started out as a straightforward offer of a major gift soon became complicated. As we began to prepare the proposal, we found that the award program did not "fit" with existing programs at our institution. We found that the faculty was not enthusiastic about administering a program from which they would derive no direct benefit. As a result, the proposal contained a number of qualifications and limitations designed to ameliorate faculty concerns. In the end the proposal provided the information requested, however, it was neither persuasive nor enthusiastic.

When we presented the proposal to Mrs. Gordon, she asked for a number of modifications. While those changes were totally understandable from her perspective, the faculty objected to a number of her requests. Rather than inform her of the faculty concerns, we attempted to finesse Mrs. Gordon's and the faculty's concerns in a second draft of the proposal. Once more, we presented Mrs. Gordon with this document.

This set the stage for six months of difficult negotiations that never got on the right track. The lack of faculty enthusiasm for the project was never adequately addressed, leading Mrs. Gordon to feel unappreciated and confused. In addition, through her many friends, she heard conflicting stories about what we really wanted to accomplish. The faculty became frustrated because they felt they were being pushed by "the administration" to be part of something they did not support. Only later did we realize that everybody was feeling pushed to do something against their nature. Our faculty was being pushed to support an ill-presented concept. Mrs. Gordon was being asked to support a program design that was not what she envisioned.

This "back and forth" might still be going on were it not for Mrs. Gordon's grace and style. As year end approached, she realized that we were all going down the wrong path, and told us so. Rather than continue the forced discussions, Mrs. Gordon decided to make a number of year-end gifts in her late husband's memory. In addition, she told us that she planned to continue her practice of supporting a large number of projects, and to take joy in seeing all those activities flourish. The major gift would not be consummated, but we could count on her continued support for a wide range of projects at our institution.

Lessons learned. There are a number of things to be learned from this case. In trying to be responsive to a friend's interest, we lost sight of our real needs and priorities. We allowed an unproven idea to replace many years of established giving patterns. Although the practice is very tempting, it is never wise to let gifts shape your institution's needs or practices.

Rather than being forthright in addressing faculty concerns, we tried to finesse them, leading to a weak and fundamentally unsound proposal. In the end, this caused the faculty, Mrs. Gordon, and the development staff to feel pushed, and colored the gift in a disingenuous light.

Finally, we forgot the importance of personal relationships. We allowed a misdirected proposal to take precedence over a set of rewarding personal re-lationships, many of which had been in existence for many years. In this case, we forgot almost all of the "basics."

Mr. and Mrs. Burke

Scenario. For many years, Mr. Burke was a regional volunteer for our institution. He was active in our campaign, and had made a major gift to support student scholarships.

Mr. and Mrs. Burke had recently lost their oldest son to a lengthy battle with kidney disease. They and their children (all grown) were investigating ways to provide a lasting memorial to their son and brother. In this effort, the Burkes were considering various gift opportunities, including establishing a hospital in their own neighborhood. Mr. Burke mentioned their personal investigation to the university's regional director, who encouraged him and his family include the university in their special giving considerations. From the to start, Mr. Burke clearly indicated that designating the recipient of their support would be a family decision.

Over the years, the university had been very careful in its cultivation of Mr. and Mrs. Burke. To strengthen the Burke's relationship with the university, development staff and university leadership had ensured that Mr. and Mrs. Burke met many of the university's top administrators. In addition, the university invited Mr. Burke to be a trustee of the university's foundation. While the elder Burkes had developed meaningful ties with the university, a close relationship had not developed between the university and the Burke children.

Understanding the Burke's interest in making a gift that would help people and honor their son, we looked for ways that our institution could help the Burkes fulfill these wishes. The university invited Mr. and Mrs. Burke and their children to campus to meet with individuals actively involved in the university's kidney disease research programs. Quickly, the lead administrator of this program was able to develop a relationship with members of the Burke family, which grew further through frequent phone contact and a personal visit to their home.

Through this relationship and contact with other members of the program and the university, the Burkes decided that the university's work in kidney disease research and treatment matched well with their giving objectives. When we presented them with the opportunity to give, the Burkes responded favorably: they provided a major gift that included support for laboratory equipment and research program endowments. The university recognized their special gift by naming a laboratory wing in memory of the Burke's late son and brother.

Lessons learned. From this example we learned that donors develop a close attachment to the purpose of their support. Receiving a major gift may rely solely on the ability of the donor to find a purpose for his or her gift in your institution. The Burke case also illustrates the importance of involving family members in the cultivation process. Only after we introduced the Burke children to the important medical research and treatment activities of our university did real giving considerations manifest themselves.

Attention to the "basics," especially as it applies to recognizing and involving the family, played a major role in this successful solicitation.

The Smith family

Scenario. The members of the Smith family were longtime supporters of the university. Both Mr. and Mrs. Smith were alumni of our university, as was one of their children. Smith family members attended many campus events. Over many years, the Smiths provided gifts in response to various annual fund requests.

A newly appointed dean became interested in getting to know the Smiths better. The dean had learned that the Smith's family business was related to the curriculum of the dean's school. As a result, the dean suspected that the Smith family might have a potential interest in his school and invited them to serve on the school's advisory board. The Smith's involvement on the advisory board brought them to campus for numerous meetings and events. Most important, by offering their advice and guidance, the Smith's became personally involved in the school's and the university's future.

In addition to their involvement with the advisory board, the Smiths had discussed with the planned giving office various charitable estate planning models that might meet their personal needs. These conversations led the Smiths to have a close relationship with the planned giving officer. As the discussion regarding their estate plans and income protection issues progressed, it became clear that the Smiths were prospects for a leadership gift to the school.

113

The dean invited the Smiths to lunch along with a key major donor volunteer (who had been a classmate of the Smiths) and the planned giving officer. During the lunch meeting, the Smiths were presented with a multi-million dollar proposal to endow a research program. Discussion continued regarding various ways to pledge and contribute the amount solicited. The volunteer expressed his satisfaction with the major gifts he had given to the university. The dean described his vision of a program that was of interest to the Smiths and would benefit the community at large. Within a month, the Smiths responded positively to the solicitation. They did not choose any of the planned gift opportunities, but instead elected to make outright gifts.

Lessons learned. In this example, the key to receiving the major gift was making the Smiths feel that they were "insiders" at our university. While much was gained at the outset by the fact that the Smiths were alumni, their "insider" status was strengthened by their association with university leadership and their experience on the advisory board.

Personal relationships went far in turning the Smith's interest and involvement into a major gift. The dean developed a personal relationship with them. The major donor volunteer involved in the solicitation was both respected and admired by the Smiths. This volunteer offered personal testimony concerning the value and satisfaction of giving to our university. The Smith's relationship with our planned giving officer allowed for an open and trusted exchange of issues and methods of giving.

As in the previous example of the Johnsons, we stuck to the "basics," and consequently obtained a significant gift to the university.

Conclusion

These case studies show that success in securing major gifts depends upon building strong relationships with potential donors. These relationships can only grow through personal involvement in the life of your institution and its people.

In building these relationships, it is essential that we recognize and respect the unique characteristics and needs of each individual donor. However, this view must never supplant our aim of maintaining the integrity of our institution. In each of the successful solicitations cited here, we were able to act on a long-standing relationship to match the interest of the donor with a priority of the university. The "fit" was not forced in order to secure a gift. As a result, the gifts were both beneficial to our university and satisfying to the donors.

The exception, of course, was the case of the Gordons in which their desire to establish a "Nobel for Art" did not match a priority of the school. The fact that we had to finesse parts of the proposal for this gift was a clear indication that our institution could not meet Mrs. Gordon's needs. We could have better shown our respect for the Gordons and our appreciation for their support by stating the worthiness of their idea but acknowledging that we could not do it justice.

The lesson from this case is clear: if we build relationships with our donors that are based on trust and respect, then we or they will be able to say "no" to a gift or a proposal without irreparably damaging the friendship or our efforts to secure major gifts for our institutions.

Chapter 15

Stewardship of Major Donors

William R. Haden
Vice President for Public Affairs
Reed College
Portland, Oregon

M ore than 20 years ago, I became acquainted with the following two concepts in educational fund raising. They have been valid and invaluable guides ever since:

1. Once a donor has made a gift of substance to your organization, it is vitally important for them to receive confirmation that they have done the right thing in making the gift.

2. The best prospect for a gift is someone who has already made one to your organization.

The relative simplicity of these two points does not detract from their efficacy. Moreover, they remind us of the essential connection between stewardship and successful solicitations.

This chapter will review how to ensure that these two straightforward concepts are constantly applied and monitored in the stewardship process. It will also show how good stewardship will attract future gifts to your institution.

Implementing the tenets of stewardship

To employ these stewardship tenets effectively, a development office or organization should ensure that the following elements are present in the development effort:

- a system or methodology for tracking of stewardship activity; and
- an interest in and a sense of caring for donors and their involvement with the institution.

Tracking systems

The first of these, a tracking system or methodology, is key to sustaining an effective stewardship program. The scope and complexity of your system should reflect the complexity of your overall development effort, the extent of your major gift program, and your institution's fund-raising needs. Tracking systems can range from "back of the envelope" lists maintained by the chief development officer to a computer-based system, which tracks thousands of major gift donors.

Several factors can guide the growth and management of an effective stewardship tracking system:

1. The size of the major donor pool. Common sense tells us that tracking 100 donors and their contact with the institution is significantly different from doing the same with 5,000 donors. Your stewardship tracking system should match the size of your donor pool.

2. The complexity of your institution's structure. A large university with multiple academic units and professional schools will require a more elaborate tracking system than a small liberal arts college. The purpose of the smaller institution's tracking system is no less important than that of the larger institution. However, the methodology for tracking donors will be less complex for the smaller institution.

3. The variety and scope of institutional gift objectives. Your institution may possess major gifts in the form of endowments, planned gifts, named facilities, and scholarships. Institutions with varied and numerous gift opportunities require more complex stewardship activities for sorting and tracking.

4. The accessibility of the tracking system and its information. The utility of a tracking system is determined by its availability and accessibility to staff and volunteers. "User-friendly" software and modest technical training for staff and volunteers will increase significantly the accessibility of your tracking system.

A sense of caring for donors

The second principle of successful stewardship should inculcate a sense of caring for donors in an institution's volunteers and staff. The president, trustees, officers, staff, faculty, and all who labor for the alma mater should nurture this caring state of mind. Stewardship finds its most meaningful expression in the willingness of these individuals to invest their time and energy in caring for donors. When an institution's leadership is committed to involving and engaging donors, that institution is well on the way toward an effective stewardship program.

Keeping donors informed and engaged

Reporting to donors, in writing or in person, is the essence of stewardship. Reports provide the assurance that donors seek: that they have done the right thing in making a major gift. While there are many methods of communicating with donors, three reporting methods are particularly effective:

1. General and focused annual reports. Though general annual reports should be sent to all major donors, they are most effective when they are personalized for each donor. Simply sending major donors a general report will not suffice. Each donor should also receive a focused annual report about the impact of his or her specific gift.

Focused reports can take many forms. Use your imagination. For example, you could provide a scholarship donor with information on the current year's scholarship recipients. Such a report could include letters of gratitude from the scholarship recipients, which discuss how the scholarship has contributed to their education and their lives. Donors of a facility might enjoy learning that their gift has helped recruit a prominent professor or researcher, elevated a department's ranking, or increased enrollment. If a facility, program, or scholarship student favorably impresses another donor, ask that donor to write a short note expressing his or her impressions to the donor responsible for the gift.

Less formal messages can supplement scheduled reports. Such messages may pass on favorable comments on a facility or program from a visiting scholar or a group of touring students.

2. Periodic meetings or gatherings of prospect groups. You may want to hold meetings and gatherings for prospects who have made similar gifts, such as scholarship donors or book fund donors. By meeting with donors who made similar gifts, donors receive confirmation of the validity and value of their gifts. These gatherings encourage informal alliances among donors interested in taking further action to support their particular area of interest. These meetings can also provide opportunities for donors to meet with those individuals benefitting from their generosity, such as scholarship recipients and academic chairs.

3. Regular meetings of major donors with key officials, faculty, and volunteers. Regular meetings of your institution's leadership and major donors can be valuable communication arenas for a successful stewardship program.

Your institution's president and other leaders should meet regularly with your most significant donors. It is especially important to invite professorship donors, other endowment donors, and building donors to regular meetings.

Words to the wise

Several pitfalls can hinder even the best intentioned stewardship program. Often small, expanding major gift efforts create habits that can hurt these programs later. In the first rush of enthusiasm over an increase in the size and number of gifts, fund raisers may give the first major donors a level of attention that will be difficult to maintain. As the number and size of the gifts continue to grow, staff can become bogged down with these earlier, indulgent stewardship practices. When establishing the elements of your stewardship program, consider the resources you will need to sustain the program in the future.

The purpose of a stewardship program is to actively appreciate donors and their gifts, while assuring them that making these gifts was worthy and right. As stewardship congratulates, it does so with an eye toward the next gift. To this end, it is essential that the relationship between stewardship and solicitation is flexible, but constant.

There is no magic in the stewardship process; it is a systematic, organized activity geared to reporting, informing, and assuring. The stewardship process may not be as glamorous as asking for a multimillion dollar gift, but it is a vital, integral part of any successful development program. Without effective steward-ship, your development program will not be able to build on its accomplishments or expand its results.

Bibliography of Major Donor Research Resources

Print sources

ABMS Compendium of Certified Medical Specialists. Evanston, IL: American Board of Medical Specialists, 1992. Provides information on over 367,000 certified doctors and medical specialists. Includes name, office address, phone, year and place of birth, educational information, type of specialty, certifications, and memberships.

Agricultural and Veterinary Sciences International Who's Who. Detroit, MI: Gale Research Co., 1992. Provides biographical profiles of nearly 75,000 agricultural and veterinary scientists from 100 countries.

Alphabetic Filing Rules. Prairie Village, KS: ARMA International, 1986. Provides authoritative treatment of standard rules for alphabetic filing, and describes and illustrates each rule in detail. Includes appendices, a bibliography, and an index. American National Standards Institute accredits this publication as an American National Standard.

American Almanac of Jobs and Salaries. by John W. Wright and Edward Dwyer. New York, NY: Avon Books, 1991. Provides information on jobs and the salaries associated with them.

The American Prospector: Contemporary Issues in Prospect Research. Rockville, MD: The Taft Group/The American Prospect Research Association, 1991.

American Women Managers and Administrators: A Selective Biographical Dictionary. Westport, CT: Greenwood Publishing Co., 1985. Includes name, biographical, and career information for 225 contemporary women who have held leadership positions in business and industry.

Annual Register of Grant Support. Wilmette, IL: National Register Publishing Co., 1992. Lists current sources of grant support with a special focus on programs offering grants to individuals for study and travel. Includes name, address, phone, major interests, eligibility requirements, and application procedures.

Arizona Foundation Directory. Phoenix, AZ: The Junior League, 1991. Profiles over 100 private and community foundations located in the state of Arizona.

Arts and Cultural Funding Report. Arlington, VA: Education Funding Research Council, 1992. For a monthly subscription, provides information on current federal and private grant sources for the arts.

The Associates Program. New York, NY: The Foundation Center, 1993. Membership in this program provides toll-free telephone reference service (up to 10 calls per month) and photocopying of Foundation Center research materials, including IRS 990PF and computerized searches. For membership information contact: Foundation Center Reference Collection, 79 Fifth Avenue, New York NY 10003.

Bank Directory of New England. Boston, MA: Shawmut Bank, 1985. Published annually, contains information on commercial and savings banks in New England. Includes bank name, address, phone number, names of officers and directors, and financial information.

Biographical Dictionaries and Related Works. Detroit, MI: Gale Research, 1986. Guide to approximately 16,000 biographical references and publications.

Biographical Dictionary of American Business Leaders. Westport, CT: Greenwood Publishing Co., 1985. Provides profiles of approximately 1,000 individuals from American business dating from early United States history to contemporary times.

Biography and Genealogy Master Index. Detroit, MI: Gale Research, 1993. Indexes the availability and location of biographical sketches in numerous biographical dictionaries.

Blue Book of Canadian Business. Toronto, Ontario: Canadian Newspaper Services International, 1992. Includes listings for 2,500 Canadian firms, including 100 listings with full details.

Britain's Privately Owned Companies: The Top 4,000. Bristol, England: Jordan & Sons, 1992. Covers 4,000 privately owned British companies. Entries include address, phone number, name of chief executives, line of business information, as well as financial statements. Available by subscription.

British Sources of Information. London, England: Routledge, 1987. Lists libraries, government offices, special collections, museums, and other organizations that are sources of information on British funders.

Business Who's Who in Australia. Crows Nest, Australia: Riddle Publishing, 1992. Provides information on approximately 9,000 Australian industrial firms, including business name, address, phone, branch operations locations, directors, key personnel, sales volume, and products and services.

Canadian Directory to Foundations. Toronto, Canada: Canadian Centre for Philanthropy, 1985. Profiles over 650 Canadian foundations and 50 American foundations that make grants within Canada. Entries include foundation name, address, key executives, funding intents, financial data, and application procedures.

Celebrity Register. Rockville, MD: The Taft Group, 1990. Lists prominent individuals in theater, dance, music, journalism, publishing, education, and government.

Chicago's Corporate Foundations: A Directory. by Ellen Dick. Oak Park, IL: Ellen Dick Libraries, 1990. Provides basic information on over 100 foundations located in the Chicago area.

Citizen's Handbook of Private Foundations in New Orleans, Louisiana. New Orleans, LA: Greater New Orleans Foundation, 1987. Directory of 112 foundations located in New Orleans.

Colorado Foundation Directory. Denver, CO: Junior League of Denver, 1990. Contains information on about 250 foundations and their giving activities during fiscal years 1986-1989.

Complete Guide to Florida Foundations. Miami, FL: John L. Adams & Company, 1990. Contains information on over 1,000 Florida-based foundations obtained from IRS 990PF returns, annual reports, and survey responses.

Connecticut Foundation Directory. Hartford, CT: D.A.T.A., Inc., 1990. Lists Connecticut foundations. Includes subject and geographic indexes.

Connecticut and Rhode Island Directory of Manufacturers. Midland Park, NJ: Commerce Register, 1993. Lists about 8,000 industrial firms with eight or more employees. Information provided includes company name, address, phone number, names of principal executives, product descriptions, number of employees, and sales profiles.

Contacts Influential. Contacts Influential Marketing Services, 1818 Wooddale Drive, Suite, Saint Paul, MN 55125-2940, (612) 731-4668. Hands-on business directory that provides access to information on key personnel.

Contemporary Theatre, Film, and Television: A Continuance of Who's Who in the Theatre. Detroit, MI: Gale Research Co., 1982. Contains 700 biographies of important figures in contemporary theatre. Published annually as a complementary volume to Who's Who in the Theatre.

Corporate 500: The Directory of Corporate Philanthropy. San Francisco, CA: Public Management Institute, 1992. Includes corporate name, corporate foundation name, address, philanthropic interests and priorities, contact person, officers, trustees, sample grants, and application procedures.

Corporate Foundation Profiles. New York, NY: The Foundation Center, 1992. Provides data on nearly 900 company-sponsored foundations with assets of $1 million or annual giving of over $100,000.

Corporate Giving Directory. Rockville, MD: The Taft Group/Fund Raising Institute, 1992. Contains information on approximately 570 of the largest corporate giving programs in the nation.

Corporate Giving Yellow Pages. Rockville, MD: The Taft Group, 1992. Lists over 3,600 contact people for corporate giving programs and corporation foundations in the United States.

Corporate Philanthropy in New England. New Haven, CT: Development and Technical Assistance Center, 1991. Lists New England corporations with gross sales over $10 million or that have at least 200 employees. Separate editions are issued for Connecticut, Maine, New Hampshire, Rhode Island and Vermont.

Delaware Foundations. Wilmington, DE: United Way of Delaware, 1979. Lists descriptions of Deleware foundations based on IRS returns and information supplied by the foundations.

Developing and Operating a Records Retention Program Guideline. Prairie Village, KS: ARMA International, 1986. Outlines program principles, staff and management structures, and program development strategies. Highlights how to determine records retention periods and obtain approval for retention schedules and procedures. Eight appendices contain samples of policy statements, destruction authorization forms, legal requirements, and other forms. Also includes a glossary and bibliography.

Directory of Biomedical and Health Care Grants. Phoenix, AZ: Oryx Press, 1990. Covers over 2,000 federal, state, and private grant funding programs in the health and medical fields. Includes contact name, address, description, giving requirements, and applications guidelines for agencies listed.

Directory of Charitable Trusts and Foundations for Hawaii's NonProfit Organizations. Honolulu, HI: Volunteer Information and Referral Service, 1990. Profiles 81 Hawaiian nonprofit organizations as well as 44 foundations based in Hawaii.

Directory of Corporate Affiliations. Wilmette, IL: National Register Publishing Co., 1992. For each corporation, lists name of parent company, address, phone number, assets, earnings, liabilities, number of employees, major plant and subsidiary locations, and names of key personnel.

Directory of Delaware Grantmakers. Wilmington, DE: Delaware Community Foundation/United Way of Delaware, 1990. Contains information on 62 foundations located in Delaware.

Directory of Directors Canada. Toronto, Ontario: The Financial Post Publications, 1992. Lists over 16,000 directors and key personnel who are Canadian residents. Also lists about 1,900 Canadian firms and their directors. Entries include name, address, executive position, education, date of birth, and directorships held.

Directory of Directors: United Kingdom Corporations. East Grinstead, England: Reed Information Services, 1992. Lists over 60,000 directors of 16,000 public and private corporations in the United Kingdom.

Directory of Directors in the City of New York and Tri-State Area. Southport, CT: Directory of Directors, 1992. Alphabetical listing of name, address, and corporate affiliation for important executives in New York City and State, New Jersey, and Connecticut. Includes a geographical index.

Directory of Foundations of the Greater Washington Area. Washington, DC: Community Foundation of Greater Washington, 1991. Contains profiles on over 500 Washington, DC-area foundations.

Directory of Grants in the Humanities. Phoenix, AZ: Oryx Press, 1990. Lists funding programs for research and performance in the liberals arts, including literature, linguistics, anthropology, religion, music, painting and theater arts.

Directory of Grants in the Physical Sciences. Phoenix, AZ: Oryx Press, 1987. Lists federal, state, corporate, and foundation sources of grants for studies in engineering, physics, math, agriculture, and computer sciences.

Directory of Idaho Foundations. Caldwell, ID: Caldwell Public Library, 1990. Based on information obtained from 1988 and 1989 IRS 990PF returns and surveys on 123 foundations and corporations with a history of giving in Idaho.

Directory of Illinois Foundations. Minnetonka, MN: Foundation Center Data, 1990. Profiles about 2,000 foundations based on IRS and survey data.

Directory of Indiana Donors. Indianapolis, IN: Donors Alliance, 1989. Profiles about 475 Indiana foundations, trusts, and scholarship programs.

Directory of International Corporate Giving in America and Abroad. Rockville, MD: The Taft Group, 1992. Profiles more than 500 companies that give in the U.S. and overseas. Gives contact person, as well as description information on foreign-owned firms that donate to institutions in the United States.

Directory of Japanese Giving. New York, NY: The Foundation Center, 1991. Entries include contact name, address, and application guidelines for 180 Japanese corporate grantmakers.

Directory of Kansas Foundations. Topeka, KS: Topeka Public Library Foundation Center, 1989. Provides information on 300 foundations and trusts located in Kansas.

Directory of Maine Foundations. Portland, ME: University of Southern Maine Office of Sponsored Research, 1990. Profiles 50 Maine-based foundations.

Directory of New England Manufacturers. Boston, MA: George D. Hall Co., 1989. Lists manufacturers in Connecticut, Maine, Massachusetts, New Hampshire, Rhode Island, and Vermont. Includes company name, address, phone number, names of principal executives, and number of employees.

Directory of Pennsylvania Foundations. Springfield, PA: Triadvocates Press in cooperation with the Free Library of Philadelphia, 1992. Provides detailed profiles of 1,000 foundations and basic information on 1,300 others in the state of Pennsylvania.

Directory of Research Grants. Phoenix, AZ: Oryx Press, 1991. Contains over 6,000 sources of research funding from federal and foundation sources.

Directory of Texas Manufacturers. Austin, TX: University of Texas. Graduate School of Business. Bureau of Business Research, 1992. Database containing information on 16,000 manufacturers operating within the state of Texas. Includes company name, address, phone number, key personnel, number of employees, sales volume, and SIC codes.

Directory of Texas Wholesalers. Austin, TX: University of Texas. Graduate School of Business. Bureau of Business Research, 1992. Contains information on wholesalers located in Texas. Includes company name, address, phone number, number of employees, sales volume, and SIC codes.

Directory of Women Entrepreneurs. Atlanta, GA: Wind River Publications, 1992. Lists over 3,000 women-owned businesses and companies with women's professional development programs or minority business assistance offices.

Dun & Bradstreet's Million Dollar Directory. Parsippany, NJ: The Dun & Bradstreet Corporation, 1992. Revised annually, this three-volume set gives financial information and names officers and directors for about 50,000 major U.S. corporations.

Dun & Bradstreet Reference Book of Corporate Managements. Parsippany, NJ: Dun & Bradstreet Corp., 1992. Contains biographical sketches on 200,000 officers, directors, and managers in nearly 12,000 corporations.

Dun's Directory of Service Companies. Parsippany, NJ: The Dun & Bradstreet Corporation, 1992. Provides information on the 50,000 largest service enterprises in the United States.

Education Grant Guides. New York, NY: The Foundation Center, 1992.

> ***Elementary & Secondary Education Guide***. Provides information on grants to elementary and secondary schools for academic programs, scholarships, counseling, educational testing, drop-out prevention, teacher training, salary support, student activities, and school libraries.

> ***Higher Education Guide***. Provides information on grants to higher education and graduate/professional schools, as well as academic libraries and student services and organizations.

> ***Libraries & Information Services Guide***. Lists grants for public, academic, special, and school libraries, as well as archives and information centers, consumer information, and philanthropy information centers.

> ***Literacy, Reading & Adult/Continuing Education Guide***. Lists grants available to organizations supporting literacy, reading, and adult basic and continuing education.

> ***Scholarships, Student Aid & Loans Guide***. Provides information on grants to organizations that give scholarships and student aid for study at undergraduate colleges and universities, medical and dental schools, nursing schools, music and art schools, cultural organizations, vocational and technical schools, and social service organizations.

Science & Technology Programs Guide. Lists grants for education and research in science and technology, scientific societies, associations and institutes, science museums, planetariums, and libraries.

Social & Political Science Programs Guide. Lists grants supporting research and education in political science, anthropology, sociology, psychology, economics, behavioral science, population studies, international studies, ethnic studies, women's studies, urban and rural studies, poverty studies, and law.

Encyclopedia of Associations. Detroit, MI: Gale Research, 1992. A guide to over 30,000 national and international organizations.

Faith and Philanthropy in America. First Edition. San Francisco, CA: Jossey-Bass Inc., 1990. Describes, through narrative and financial analysis, the relationship between religious commitment and charitable activity.

Filing Procedures Guideline. Prairie Village, KS: ARMA International, 1989. Guideline of filing procedures for active paper records, magnetic media, and micrographic media. Provides a reference for storing and retrieving active records. Includes a bibliography, glossary, and index.

Florida Manufacturer's Register. Chicago, IL: The Manufacturers News, 1990. Provides information on Florida manufacturers. Lists manufacturers alphabetically and by product or industrial service, SIC codes, computer system, and geographic location.

Foundation Directory. New York, NY: The Foundation Center, 1992. Contains entries for over 6,000 foundations with assets of $1 million or annual giving of $100,000.

Foundation Grants Index. New York, NY: The Foundation Center, 1992. Contains state-by-state listings of over 40,000 grants of $5,000 or more awarded by over 400 foundations.

Foundation Grants to Individuals. New York, NY: The Foundation Center, 1991. Provides information on over 2,000 independent and corporate foundations.

Foundation Guide: Northeast Florida. Jacksonville, FL: Volunteer Jacksonville, 1990. Contains information on 50 foundations located in northeast Florida.

Fund Raisers Guide to Human Service Funding. Rockville, MD: The Taft Group, 1992. Lists corporations and foundations that make grants to human service projects.

Fund Raisers Guide to Religious Philanthropy. Rockville, MD: Taft Group/ Fund Raising Institute, 1992. Provides profiles and giving histories for approximately 400 foundations that make donations to religious causes.

Funding Decision Makers. Rockville, MD: The Taft Group, 1992. Lists over 15,000 decision makers who determine the recipients for foundation and corporate giving. Includes a listing of board affiliations with other organizations.

Georgia Manufacturer's Register. Chicago, IL: The Manufacturers News, 1990. Provides information on Georgia manufacturers. Lists manufacturers alphabetically and by product or industrial service, SIC codes, computer system, and geographic location.

Grant Seekers Guide. Mount Kisco, NY: Moyer Bell, 1989. Profiles 450 sources of grants for nonprofit organizations working in areas such as the environment, women's issues, AIDS, and other causes.

Grants for Libraries: A Guide To Public and Private Funding Programs and Proposal Writing Techniques. Englewood, CO: Libraries Unlimited, 1986. Lists funding groups for academic, public, and private libraries, as well as for library and information science education.

Guide to Arkansas Funding Sources. Hampton, AR: Independent Community Consultants, 1990. Contains information on 108 Arkansas foundations.

Guide to California Foundations. San Francisco, CA: Northern California Grantmakers, 1988. Lists over 800 foundations located in California that make grants of over $40,000 per year.

Guide to Corporate Giving in the Arts. New York, NY: American Council for the Arts, 1987. Lists corporations providing funding in the arts.

Guide to Private Fortunes. Rockville, MD: The Taft Group, 1992. Includes profiles of 1,250 of the wealthiest and most philanthropic individuals in the United States.

Guide to Santa Clara Foundations. San Jose, CA: Nonprofit Development Center, 1990. Lists 19 foundations headquartered in Santa Clara County.

Gulf Coast Industrial Handbook: Florida, Alabama, Mississippi, Louisiana, Texas. Houston, TX: CISMAP, 1992. Lists 1,000 Gulf Coast industrial plants, such as refineries, steel plants, power plants, and chemical plants. Includes plant name, address, phone number, and key personnel.

Harris Industrial Directories. Twinsburg, OH: Harris Publishing Company, 1993. Lists corporate and product data on manufacturing companies located in Illinois, Kentucky, Michigan, Ohio, Pennsylvania, and West Virginia. Includes names and titles of key executives. Arranged alphabetically, geographically, and by product code.

Hispanics and the Nonprofit Sector. New York, NY: The Foundation Center, 1991. Chronicles the history of Hispanic nonprofit organizations from the mutualistas of the 19th century to modern funding responses, such as the National Council of La Raza and the Mexican American Legal Defense Fund.

Hoover's Handbook of American Businesses. Austin, TX: The Reference Press, 1992. Provides profiles of major United States businesses.

How to Look It Up Online. New York, NY: St. Martin's Press, 1987. Contains an overview of commercial online databases with comparisons, analyses, and searching tips.

Illinois Manufacturer's Register. Chicago, IL: The Manufacturers News, 1990. Provides information on Illinois manufacturers. Lists manufacturers alphabetically and by product or industrial service, SIC codes, computer system, and geographic location.

Index of Private Foundations. Baltimore, MD: Maryland Attorney General's Office, 1989. Profiles over 550 Maryland foundations.

Indiana Manufacturer's Register. Chicago, IL: The Manufacturers News, 1990. Provides information on Indiana manufacturers. Lists manufacturers alphabetically and by product or industrial service, SIC codes, computer system, and geographic location.

Inside Japanese Support. Rockville, MD: The Taft Group, 1992. Provides contact names, application information, program descriptions, lists of representative grants, identities of 280 United States subsidiaries of Japanese firms, and profiles of 40 Japan-based foundations.

International Directory of Company Histories. Detroit, MI: Gale Research Company, 1986. Presents basic information and company histories for 1,200 leading companies located in the United States, Great Britain, Europe, and Japan.

International Directory of Corporate Affiliations. Wilmette, IL: National Register Publishing Company, 1992. Guide to the ownership of international corporations. Includes information regarding the ownership of more than 1,000 foreign companies, as well as 17,000 subsidiaries, divisions, and affiliates in the United States. Also includes information on 1,400 American companies and their 13,000 overseas subsidiaries.

International Foundation Directory. Detroit, MI: Gale Research Company, 1974. Profiles selected national foundations from around the world, including more than 700 institutions in 49 countries. Emphasizes foundations, trusts, and other nonprofit organizations operating on an international basis.

International Who's Who 1988-89. Detroit, MI: Gale Research Company, 1988. Lists more than 18,000 prominent personalities. Includes biographical information on individuals in international affairs, government, diplomacy, sports, and the arts.

International Who's Who of Professional Business Women. Cambridge, England: International Biographical Centre, 1989. Includes biographical sketches of over 5,000 leading female executives.

Iowa Directory of Foundations. Estes Park, CO: Trumpet Associates, 1984. Profiles 250 Iowa foundations.

Iowa Manufacturer's Register. Chicago, IL: The Manufacturers News, 1990. Provides information on Iowa manufacturers. Lists manufacturers alphabetically and by product or industrial service, SIC codes, computer system, and geographic location.

Japanese Corporate Connection: A Guide for Fundraisers. New York, NY: The Foundation Center, 1991.

Kentucky Manufacturer's Register. Chicago, IL: The Manufacturers News, 1990. Provides information on Kentucky manufacturers. Lists manufacturers alphabetically and by product or industrial service, SIC codes, computer system, and geographic location.

Macmillan Directory of Leading Private Companies. Wilmette, IL: National Register Publishing Co., 1991. Lists over 7,000 privately owned companies. Includes company name, address, phone number, financial assets and liabilities, net worth, approximate sales, and key personnel.

MacRae's Industrial Directory: Connecticut and Rhode Island. New York, NY: MacRae's Blue Book, 1992. Lists key information on nearly 5,000 firms located in Connecticut and Rhode Island.

MacRae's Industrial Directory: Maine, New Hampshire, and Vermont. New York, NY: MacRae's Blue Book, 1992. Provides key information on 3,500 industrial firms located in Maine, New Hampshire, and Vermont.

MacRae's Industrial Directory: Massachusetts and Rhode Island. New York, NY: MacRae's Blue Book, 1992. Provides key information on 8,500 industrial firms located in Massachusetts and Rhode Island.

Maine, Vermont, and New Hampshire Directory of Manufacturers. Midland Park, NJ: Commerce Register Inc., 1990. Provides information on manufacturers located in Maine, Vermont, and New Hampshire. Lists manufacturers alphabetically and by product or industrial service, SIC codes, computer system, and geographic location.

Martindale-Hubbell Law Directory. Summit, NJ: Martindale-Hubbell, 1992. Lists major law firms and lawyers located in the United States. Includes brief biographical descriptions and listings of representative clients.

Mass High Tech Directory of Connecticut & Rhode Island High Tech Companies. Watertown, MA: Mass High Tech, 1991. Lists high tech and software development companies in Connecticut and Rhode Island. Includes company name, address, phone number, key executives, number of employees, and product and service information.

Massachusetts Grantmakers. Boston, MA: Associated Grantmakers of Massachusetts, 1990. Describes approximately 440 Massachusetts foundations and corporate giving programs.

Medical and Healthcare Marketplace Guide. Philadelphia, PA: MLR Biomedical Information Services, 1975. Lists over 5,000 companies that do business in the medical and health fields.

Medical Research Funding Directory. New York, NY: Science Support Center, 1992. Bulletin published three times per month listing 20 to 35 federal contracts available in health research and 15 to 40 grants from both federal and private sources with deadlines in the coming two-month period.

Michigan Foundation Directory: Including Listings of Corporate Giving and a Survey of Michigan Foundation Philanthropy. Grand Haven, MI: Council of Michigan Foundations, 1988. Lists 475 corporate and foundation programs with assets of $200,000 or grant making of $25,000 operating within the state of Michigan. Includes a list of public foundations that redistribute monies raised from the public.

Million Dollar Directory: America's Leading Public and Private Companies. Parsippany, NJ: The Dun & Bradstreet Corporation, 1992. Provides information on more than 160,000 of America's largest companies. Five volumes include information on executives, company size, and line of business.

Minnesota Manufacturer's Register. Chicago, IL: The Manufacturers News, 1990. Provides information on Minnesota manufacturers. Lists manufacturers alphabetically and by product or industrial service, SIC codes, computer system, and geographic location.

Missouri Manufacturer's Register. Chicago, IL: The Manufacturers News, 1990. Provides information on Missouri manufacturers. Lists manufacturers alphabetically and by product or industrial service, SIC codes, computer system, and geographic location.

The Mitchell Guide to Foundations, Corporations, and Their Managers: New Jersey. Belli Mea, NJ: The Mitchell Guide, 1988. Lists over 190 foundations and 550 corporate donors in the state of New Jersey.

National Catholic Development Conference Bibliography of Fund Raising and Philanthropy. Hempstead, NY: National Catholic Development Conference, 1982. Lists over 1,000 books, services, periodicals, and publishers in the fund-raising and development fields.

National Directory of Arts and Education Support by Business Corporations. Des Moines, IA: Washington International Arts Letter, 1989. Lists private foundations and business corporations that provide funding to the arts and humanities.

National Directory of Arts Support by Private Foundations. Des Moines, IA: Washington International Arts Letter, 1990. Lists private foundations offering grants in the arts.

National Directory of Corporate Giving. New York, NY: The Foundation Center, 1991. Provides profiles on over 2,000 corporate philanthropic programs. Includes company name, address, financial data, locations of plants and subsidiaries, and charitable giving statements.

National Guide to Funding for the Environment and Animal Welfare. New York, NY: The Foundation Center, 1992. Describes foundations and grants that provide support to projects and organizations involved in international conservation, ecological research, litigation and advocacy, waste reduction, and animal welfare.

National Guide to Funding in Health. New York, NY: The Foundation Center, 1990. Lists over 4,000 foundation and corporate giving sources that award grants to hospitals and health-related organizations.

National Guide to Funding in Arts and Culture. New York, NY: The Foundation Center, 1992. Contains 3,300 profiles of grantmaking organizations that provide funding to arts and cultural programs.

National Guide to Funding in Higher Education. New York, NY: The Foundation Center, 1992. Provides information on over 3,600 foundations and corporate giving programs that award grants to higher education.

National Guide to Funding in Religion. New York, NY: The Foundation Center, 1991. Contains information on 2,800 foundations and corporate giving programs that fund churches, missionary societies, and religious welfare and education programs.

The New Jersey Corporate Guide: The Corporate Guide to New Jersey Business. Morganville, NJ: Corfacts, 1991. Provides brief profiles of companies operating in the state of New Jersey. Lists company name, address, phone number, names of key officers, and income statements.

The New Jersey Directory: The Insider Guide to New Jersey Leaders. Princeton, NJ: Joshua Communications, 1992. Contains brief biographies of key business leaders in the state of New Jersey, as well as corporate profiles for public and private businesses.

New York State Foundations. New York, NY: The Foundation Center, 1991. Lists independent, corporate, and community foundations located throughout the state of New York.

Notable American Women 1607-1950. Cambridge, MA: The Belknap Press of Harvard University, 1971.

Numeric Filing Guideline. Prairie Village, KS: ARMA International, 1989. Guide to selection and design of numeric filing systems. Lists advantages and disadvantages of consecutive, middle-digit, terminal-digit, chronologic, decimal, duplex-numeric, and block numeric filing systems. Includes appendices, a bibliography, and an index.

Official Catholic Directory. Wilmette, IL: P.J. Kennedy & Sons, Macmillan Directory Division, 1992. Lists over 60,000 clerical and lay leaders of the institutions, organizations, and possessions of the Catholic Church.

Ohio Manufacturer's Register. Chicago, IL: The Manufacturers News, 1990. Provides information on Ohio manufacturers. Lists manufacturers alphabetically and by product or industrial service, SIC codes, computer system, and geographic location.

Owners and Officers of Private Companies. Rockville, MD: The Taft Group, 1992. Provides company name, address, phone number, contact personnel, number of employees, and SIC codes for over 44,000 privately held United States firms.

Pennsylvania Manufacturer's Register. Chicago, IL: The Manufacturers News, 1990. Provides information on Pennsylvania manufacturers. Lists manufacturers alphabetically and by product or industrial service, SIC codes, computer system, and geographic location.

People Property Prospects.. Rockville, MD: The Taft Group, 1992. Provides information based on the 1990 census and public records for 40,000 homeowners within the 120 wealthiest zip codes.

Practical Guide to Planned Giving. Rockville, MD: The Taft Group, 1992. Describes planned giving laws and tax strategies.

Prospect Researcher's Guide to Biographical Research Collections. Rockville, MD: The Taft Group, 1991. Lists over 1,000 libraries and special collections maintaining subscriptions, information services, publications, and special indexes for fund raisers.

Quantus: Annual Compendium of Directors. Traverse City, MI: PC Research Service, 1992. This cross-referenced directory lists directors of leading public companies, their current job status, personal and family information, shareholdings, salary, alma mater, and other affiliations.

Records Retention Procedures. Prairie Village, KS: ARMA International, 1990. Discusses the process of determining how long to keep records, the methodology of retention programs, and some general technical records retention information.

Reference Book of Corporate Managements: America's Corporate Leaders. Parsippany, NJ: The Dun & Bradstreet Corporation, 1992. Contains biographical profiles of principal officers and directors of over 12,000 leading United States companies.

Religious Philanthropy in New England: A Sourcebook. New Haven, CT: Development and Technical Assistance Center, 1987. Lists over 500 organizations in New England with a history of funding religious groups and activities. Includes a listing of grant recipients, policies, and special provisions. Classified by denomination.

San Diego County Foundation Directory. San Diego, CA: San Diego Community Foundation, 1989. Compiles in a loose-leaf binder copies of IRS 990PF returns for 123 foundations based in San Diego County.

Scholarships and Loans for Nursing Education. New York, NY: National League for Nursing, 1992. Lists organizations that provide fellowships, grants, scholarships, and loans for nursing education. Includes names and addresses of funding sources, names of scholarships, restrictions, and application procedures.

Search & Research. Noel C. Stevenson. Salt Lake City, UT: Desert Book Company, 1977. Assists researchers in locating sources of information from public records and other resources within each state.

Standard & Poor's Register of Corporations, Directors, and Executives.
New York, NY: Standards & Poor's Corp., 1992. Includes information on over
50,000 U.S. corporations, including names and titles of 400,000 executives.

Subject Filing Guidelines. Prairie Village, KS: ARMA International, 1988. Describes dictionary and encyclopedic filing arrangements, coding systems, types
of indices, and cross-referencing procedures. Includes an appendix with sample
records analysis and inventory forms, a bibliography, and definitions.

Taft Corporate Giving Directory. Rockville, MD: The Taft Group, 1992. Details
over 500 major corporate and direct giving programs. Includes name, address,
biographical sketches of officers, board member listings, grants data, application procedures, and other information regarding specific corporations.

Taft Foundation Reporter. Rockville, MD: The Taft Group, 1992. Includes
information on 500 foundations with national and regional giving emphases.
Includes foundaton name, contact person, officers and directors, application
procedures, and information on recent grants.

Texas Manufacturer's Register. Chicago, IL: The Manufacturers News, 1990.
Provides information on Texas manufacturers. Lists manufacturers alphabetically and by product or industrial service, SIC codes, computer system, and
geographic location.

Wealth Holders of America. San Francisco, CA: Biodata, 1988. Lists political
contributions of individuals with a net worth of at least $1 million.

West Virginia Manufacturer's Register. Chicago, IL: The Manufacturers News,
1990. Provides information on West Virginia manufacturers. Lists manufacturers
alphabetically and by product or industrial service, SIC codes, computer system,
and geographic location.

***Where to Write for Vital Records: Births, Deaths, Marriages, and Di-
vorces***. Washington, DC: Dept. of Health and Human Services-National Center
for Health Statistics, 1984. Lists vital statistics offices for each state.

Who's Wealthy in America. Rockville, MD: The Taft Group, 1991. Lists name,
address, political contributions, and educational level of 100,000 wealthy
individuals living in the United States.

Who's Who Among Black Americans. Detroit, MI: Gale Research, 1991. Lists
biographical sketches for over 18,000 African-American leaders.

Who's Who Among Hispanic Americans. Detroit, MI: Gale Research, 1991.
Contains biographical profiles on prominent Hispanic individuals.

Who's Who in America. Detroit, MI: Gale Research, 1991.

Who Was Who in America. Detroit, MI: Gale Research, 1991.
  Historical Volume (1606-1896)
  Volume I (1897-1942)
  Volume II (1943-1950)
  Volume III (1951-1960)
  Volume IV (1961-1968)
  Volume V (1969-1973)
  Volume VI (1974-1976)
  Volume VII (1977-1981)
  Volume VIII(1982-1985)
  Index Volume (1607-1985)

Who's Who in Art. Detroit, MI: Gale Research Company, 1988. Contains biographical sketches on about 3,000 artists, designers, critics, writers, and curators. Particularly noted for coverage of British artists.

Who's Who in Canada. Toronto, Canada: Global Press, 1990. Contains biographical listings of leading Canadians in business, the professions, government, and academia.

Who's Who in Japan. Detroit, MI: Gale Research Company, 1987. Contains 42,000 biographical profiles on leading figures in contemporary Japan.

Who's Who in Professional and Executive Women. Philadelphia, PA: American Society of Professional and Executive Women, 1992. Includes biographical sketches of 5,000 women of distinction.

Who's Who in Technology. Detroit, MI: Gale Research Company, 1989. Contains nearly 38,000 biographical profiles on individuals in scientific fields, specifically engineering and technology.

Who's Who in the Securities Industry. Chicago, IL: Economist Publishing Co., 1989. Lists biographical sketches on approximately 1,000 investment bankers.

Who's Who in the Theatre. Detroit, MI: Gale Research Company, 1981. Contains biographies of 2,200 actors, actresses, directors, playwrights, and other figures of the stage.

Who's Who of Black Millionaires. Fresno, CA: Who's Who of Black Millionaires, 1988. Contains biographical sketches of Black Americans whose net worth is $1 million or more.

Who's Who of Canadian Women. Toronto, Canada: Trans-Canada Press, 1984. Contains biographical sketches on notable women in Canada.

Other ***Who's Who*** Sources:
  Who's Who in the World
  Who's Who in American Law
  Who's Who in Entertainment
  Who's Who in Finance and Industry
  Who's Who in the East
  Who's Who in the Midwest
  Who's Who in the South and Southwest
  Who's Who in the West
  Who's Who of American Women
  Who's Who of Emerging Leaders in America
  ***Marquis Who's Who* Index**

Wisconsin Manufacturer's Register. Chicago, IL: The Manufacturers News, 1990. Provides information on Wisconsin manufacturers. Lists manufacturers alphabetically and by product or industrial service, SIC codes, computer system, and geographic location.

On-line databases

DataTimes (Oklahoma City, OK). Contains newspapers, magazines, and business information from over 650 sources. Includes access to *Dow Jones News/ Retrieval*.

DIALOG Information Services (Palo Alto, CA). Contains over 400 databases, each maintained by initial source. Offers many specialized professional databases featuring collections such as a foundations index, foundation grants index, and national newspapers and periodicals index.

Dow Jones News/Retrieval (Princeton, NJ). Contains more than 50 different business and financial information databases. S&P's disclosure database is an important component to this Dow Jones service for the prospect researcher. Rates vary according to time of day of use, database in use, subscription plan, and modem. Educational organizations should be eligible for discount pricing for on-line connect time charges.

Dun & Bradstreet Information Services (Paramus, NJ). Subscription service important for supplying business information reports, especially regarding small and privately held businesses.

Invest/Net Group, Inc. (Ft. Lauderdale, FL). An on-line database which is updated daily providing record of all securities transactions by officers and directors of all publicly held companies. Data available from 1983 to present, and includes information on over 150,000 insiders at 10,000 U.S. companies.

About the Editors

Roy Muir

For over 25 years, Roy Muir has been active in higher education advancement in institutions ranging from liberal arts colleges to universities. Throughout his career Roy has gained extensive experience in comprehensive campaign and major gift management. He began his advancement work as director of public relations at Graceland College. Roy later worked as the associate director of alumni relations at Washington University and as director of development at the Georgetown University Medical Center.

In 1976, Roy came to the University of Michigan where, as the associate vice president for development, he is currently responsible for the university's major gift development efforts. In addition, Roy is currently associate director of the Campaign for Michigan, an ambitious campaign to raise $850 million in current gifts and $150 million in bequests for the institution. When announced in 1992, the Campaign for Michigan was the largest of its kind campaign launched by a public university.

Roy has been active in CASE programs throughout his career, and has been a regular presenter at conferences and workshops. In addition, Roy has co-chaired the CASE Winter Institute for Senior Development Officers, worked as a CASE consultant, and served on district program committees and fund-raising awards committees. Roy is currently a member of the CASE Campaign Reporting Advisory Group.

Jerry May

Jerry May, a Hope College graduate and University of Vermont master's degree holder, has not simply raised money for institutions—he has developed a long and effective career of nurturing and acquiring significant major donor support. As vice president for development at Ohio State University, Jerry directs all of the university's fund-raising efforts including policy formulation, strategic planning, program implementation, and development staff management.

Prior to his current position, Jerry was the director of major gift programs at the University of Michigan—a program that cultivated donors capable of giving $100,000 and more. As the senior associate director of the Campaign for Michigan, he effected the success of a five-year $160 million campaign.

Often a speaker at professional fund-raising events, Jerry has brought his expertise to many CASE conferences. In addition to co-chairing the CASE Winter Institute for Senior Development Officers, Jerry has also led CASE Major Gift Fund Raising and Corporate and Foundation Relations conferences.

NOTES

NOTES

NOTES

NOTES

NOTES

NOTES